IEG WORLD BANK
INDEPENDENT EVALUATION GROUP

Annual Review of

Development Effectiveness 2008

Shared Global Challenges

2008
The World Bank
Washington, D.C.

http://www.worldbank.org/ieg

HG
3881.5
.W57
E93
2008

Latest
10 yrs

This volume, except for the "Management Response" and the "Chairman's Summary," is a product of the staff of the Independent Evaluation Group of the World Bank Group. The findings, interpretations, and conclusions expressed in this volume do not necessarily reflect the views of the Executive Directors of The World Bank or the governments they represent. This volume does not support any general inferences beyond the scope of the evaluation, including any inferences about the World Bank Group's past, current, or prospective overall performance.

The World Bank Group does not guarantee the accuracy of the data included in this work. The boundaries, colors, denominations, and other information shown on any map in this work do not imply any judgement on the part of The World Bank Group concerning the legal status of any territory or the endorsement or acceptance of such boundaries.

Rights and Permissions

Cover: Indonesian elementary schoolchildren wear surgical masks in response to 2003 outbreak of SARS in China; photo ©Reuters/ Corbis, reproduced by permission. Satellite image of hurricane; photo ©Adastra/ Getty Images, reproduced by permission. Bengal tiger; photo ©DLILLC/Corbis, reproduced by permission. Wind turbine farm; photo ©Frank Whitney/ Getty Images, reproduced by permission.

ISSN: 1520-9733
ISBN-13: 978-0-8213-7714-7
e-ISBN-13: 978-0-8213-7716-1
DOI: 10.1596/978-0-8213-7714-7

World Bank InfoShop
E-mail: pic@worldbank.org
Telephone: 202-458-5454
Facsimile: 202-522-1500

Independent Evaluation Group
Knowledge Programs and Evaluation Capacity
Development (IEGKE)
E-mail: ieg@worldbank.org
Telephone: 202-458-4497
Facsimile: 202-522-3125

 Printed on Recycled Paper

Contents

Tables

Abbreviations

AfricaRMS	Africa Results Monitoring System
ARDE	Annual Review of Development Effectiveness
CAE	Country Assistance Evaluation
CAS	Country Assistance Strategy
CASCR	Country Assistance Strategy Completion Report
CGIAR	Consultative Group on International Agriculture Research
CODE	Committee on Development Effectiveness
CPS	Country Partnership Strategy
DGF	Development Grant Facility
FY	Fiscal year
GEF	Global Environment Facility
GPG	Global public good
GPP	Global programs and partnerships
IBRD	International Bank for Reconstruction and Development
ICR	Implementation Completion and Results report
IDA	International Development Association
IEG	Independent Evaluation Group
IFFIm	International Financing Facility for Vaccines and Immunization
ISR	Implementation Status and Results report
LIC	Low-income country
LICUS	Low-Income Countries Under Stress
M&E	Monitoring and evaluation
MAR	Management Action Record
MIC	Middle-income country
NGO	Nongovernmental organization
PCF	Prototype Carbon Fund
PRSC	Poverty Reduction Support Credit
QAG	Quality Assurance Group
R&D	Research and development
RMS	Results Measurement System

Acknowledgments

This report was written by Thomas O'Brien, and prepared by a team under his leadership. The team's core members were Brett Libresco, Yoshi Uchimura, Pamela Velez-Vega, Victoria Chang, and Jan Rielaender. The report draws upon significant research and contributions provided by Scott Barrett, Robin Broadfield, John Eriksson, Nidhi Khattri, Shonar Lala, Domenico Lombardi, and Andrew Waxman. Marinella Yadao and Yvette Jarencio-Lukban provided support and assistance to the team during the project. William Hurlbut edited an earlier version of the manuscript. Helen Chin edited the report for publication.

Alan Gelb, Steve Radelet, and Salvatore Schiavo-Campo served as peer reviewers of the final evaluation report.

The evaluation team greatly appreciates the time and insights from many individuals inside and outside the World Bank who were interviewed for this report. The evaluation benefited substantially from the constructive advice and feedback from many staff in the World Bank Group.

The evaluation was conducted under the guidance of Mark Sundberg, Manager, IEG Corporate and Global Evaluation and Methods Unit.

Director-General, Evaluation: *Vinod Thomas*
Director, Independent Evaluation Group, World Bank: *Cheryl Gray*
Manager, Corporate and Global Evaluation and Methods: *Mark Sundberg*
Task Manager: *Thomas O'Brien*

Indonesian elementary schoolchildren wear surgical masks in response to 2003 outbreak of SARS in China; photo ©Reuters/ Corbis, reproduced by permission.

Foreword

A farmer in Kenya faces a hopeful future as he exports to growing markets opened up by global trading agreements. But another in Vietnam stares at ruin as her poultry is culled so that the threat of avian flu can be curtailed. And others in the Bay of Bengal face longer-term danger from a growing risk of floods as the earth's climate warms. Living continents apart, these farmers have more in common than their efforts to escape poverty. Their futures are increasingly interlinked with the world's response to shared global challenges.

Such global public goods—a global trading system, biodiversity—and the issue of combating global public bads—climate change, transborder contagion—share the problem of undersupply. To increase supply, and to avoid the "tragedy of the commons," collective action is required, often with coordinated responses at the local, regional, and global levels. Where the benefits can be directly felt at the local level, such as halting transmission of diseases, motivating action is less difficult. Where fully appropriating the benefits locally is not possible or takes a long time—such as climate change—collective action is far more difficult and requires global efforts to help motivate local action.

The World Bank has set fostering global public goods as one of its six strategic priorities under its new president, and is deeply involved in efforts to strengthen their supply through investments spanning local, regional, and global public goods. This goes hand-in-hand with the Bank's commitment to delivering development results, including through the use of the new round of International Development Association funding to which donors have committed a record of nearly $42 billion.

This year's Annual Review of Development Effectiveness focuses on assessing the World Bank's development effectiveness, with special attention to global public goods. It notes some encouraging developments. Project performance has improved over the medium term; country programs have worked relatively well in several large nations that house a majority of the world's poor; and the Bank has increased attention to collective international action on global public goods and advocated effectively on some of those important challenges. But work is required to remedy weaknesses. Notably there is a need to go beyond the Bank's country-based model when tackling issues where the perceived local and national benefits of action do not match global benefits from collective action. Attention should be paid to improving weak performance of country programs in smaller states and those with extensive poverty, and redressing shortcomings in applying monitoring and evaluation in projects and country programs.

Over the next decade and beyond, the success of the international community and the World Bank Group in rising to the shared global challenges of our time will be crucial to reducing poverty and, indeed, to solving the looming challenges the world collectively faces.

Vinod Thomas
Director-General, Evaluation

Bengal tiger; photo ©DLILLC/Corbis, reproduced by permission.

Executive Summary

For the World Bank and its partners, the ever-present test is to deliver results—to lift people out of poverty and promote socially and environmentally sustainable development. Achieving such success in any individual country is increasingly intertwined with making progress on shared global challenges. A fair and efficient international trade regime, for example, is a global public good that allows developing countries to trade more and grow faster. The increasing global threat of climate change—a "public bad," by contrast—particularly imperils the poor, who bear the brunt of more frequent natural disasters and hazards to health and agriculture.

This year's Annual Review of Development Effectiveness is in a new format and presents evidence on the Bank's efforts in two important and connected areas. Part I, which is a standard section of the new format, helps to track Bank performance, notably trends in outcomes of Bank projects and country programs, the evolution of monitoring and evaluation (M&E), and the role of evaluation in the results agenda. Part II examines a special topic of great relevance to the results described in the first part: the Bank's work in fostering global public goods, such as protecting the earth's climate and preventing the spread of dangerous communicable diseases. Global public goods tend to be undersupplied, as are all public goods. Motivating local action is easier when the benefits are captured locally: efforts to stop the transborder spread of pandemic disease are more easily motivated when the results directly benefit local populations. By contrast, reducing greenhouse gas emissions is harder to motivate because of a lack of perceived local benefits, particularly in the near term. The report examines both situations, but it is the latter—where global and local benefits diverge—in which the challenges are greatest and the role of the Bank is potentially pathbreaking.

Development outcomes from Bank lending have improved over the medium term, mostly through a rise in the share of projects rated as moderately satisfactory in meeting their objectives. Achievements of country programs in meeting their objectives—typically including growth, poverty reduction, and environmental sustainability—have been moderately satisfactory or better in three-fifths of cases, including in several large countries, home to the majority of the world's poor. But too many other programs, particularly in impoverished countries, have been moderately unsatisfactory or worse. The Bank's overall approach to M&E has many strengths, including recent progress in updating its policies on lending and country strategies to emphasize M&E. Yet significant overoptimism in the Bank's self-assessment of ongoing project performance and weaknesses in the use of M&E systems are of concern. The quality of project M&E is often quite low, and results frameworks in country assistance strategies need clearer and simpler articulation with baseline indicators if they are to be effective as management tools.

The Bank has paid growing attention to global public goods, which increasingly influence development outcomes. It has helped foster global public goods through country activities, and its country model has worked well when national and global interests dovetail—often with an agreed international framework for action—and when grant finance supports country-based investments. The Bank has also been a strong advocate for changes in global systems, such as international trade reform, where it has expertise and is willing to engage in public debate. But the greatest challenges arise where local, national, and global benefits—actual or perceived, immediate or for the next generation—diverge significantly from each other. For example, the investments needed to protect the earth's climate and environmental commons vary considerably at the local, national, and global levels, as do the costs and benefits of such actions. To more effectively bridge the gap between global needs and country concerns, the Bank should consider: creating dedicated budgets and better incentives for country teams to work on global public goods; deploying its global knowledge networks more effectively; developing new financial instruments and securing additional resources, including grant funds, to support country-level investments; and using its standing more powerfully to give greater voice to developing countries in the governance of global programs.

Part I: Tracking Bank Performance

Development outcomes from Bank lending have improved over the medium term. Over the three years to end-fiscal 2007, IEG's evaluations confirm that 80 percent of projects were moderately satisfactory or better in meeting their development objectives. This meets the Bank's own performance target and is a significant improvement from the start of the decade. A Bank-supported water project in Cambodia, which brought clean water to 750,000 people in Phnom Penh, illustrates such development outcomes.

Project outcomes improved in most sectors, but average ratings slipped for projects in the fields of health and public sector governance during fiscal 2003–07, as compared with fiscal 1998–2002.

Project performance among the Bank's Regions improved most in Africa—about three-quarters of projects, weighted by disbursement, during fiscal 2003–07 were moderately satisfactory or better in meeting development objectives, as compared with 60 percent during fiscal 1998–2002. There is still a challenge for Africa projects to improve further and get closer to the performance in other Bank Regions.

Bank management should avoid overoptimism in assessing ongoing project performance to improve real-time management for results. The considerable increase, in fiscal 2007, in the difference between the Bank's self-ratings of project performance and IEG's final ratings of development outcomes (sometimes called the "disconnect") illustrates the point. In fiscal 2007, over two-thirds of projects rated moderately unsatisfactory or worse by IEG had been reported by the Bank as moderately satisfactory or better just before they closed. Such a wide disconnect—about twice as large as in fiscal 2005 and fiscal 2006—means management is less likely to identify problem projects and take timely remedial action.

Such management attention is important given that the share of projects with moderately satisfactory or better outcomes has fallen from nearly 83 percent in fiscal 2006 to 76 percent in fiscal 2007. A single year's data is not, by itself, a cause for alarm, but vigilance is needed to ensure that it does not foreshadow a persistent decline. Excessively complex project design and overly ambitious assumptions on political ownership and implementation capacity lay at the heart of many poorly performing projects that exited in fiscal 2007.

Securing strong development outcomes at the country level has proved challenging. Over the past 10 years, evaluations of 81 Bank country programs—incorporating projects, policy and technical advice, and other types of assistance—show that three-fifths of them were moderately satisfactory or better in meeting their development outcomes. Looking at specific grades on IEG's ratings scale, the Bank succeeded in supporting satisfactory outcomes in 30 percent of evaluated programs—including several large and important countries such as Brazil and China, which have made strides in reducing poverty. A further 30 percent of country programs were rated moderately satisfactory. But the remaining 40 percent of programs—concentrated in countries that are smaller or have extensive poverty, such as Malawi—were moderately unsatisfactory or worse in meeting their stated development objectives. Very few country programs are producing best-practice results. Indeed, of 36 programs rated since fiscal 2002, not one has been highly satisfactory. At the same time, no program has ever been rated highly unsatisfactory.

How well is the Bank using and learning from good monitoring and evaluation (M&E) systems, which are key to improving its effectiveness over the longer term? The Bank's overall approach to M&E has many strengths, and in recent years there has been considerable progress in updating its policies on lending and country strategies to emphasize M&E. The introduction of results-based country assistance strategies has been a particularly significant step. But considerable room for improvement remains in putting all of this into practice.

At the project level, the overall quality of M&E has been low—rated as modest or negligible in two-thirds of projects for which data are available—since fiscal 2006. Some of the factors contributing to low M&E quality assessments were poorly designed results frameworks, poorly articulated results chains linking outputs with outcomes, and performance indicators lacking baselines and targets.

Effective results frameworks at the country level are key to managing for results. While staff are gaining experience with results frameworks, too often such frameworks have been poorly formulated and hence their usefulness is undermined. In many cases, frameworks identify too many outcomes and monitoring indicators and lack baselines and targets. Their use for monitoring and managing the country program, and for informing country assistance evaluations, is very limited because of

poor design and the absence of incentives to conduct M&E. Even so, there are examples of emerging good practice such as the "Moldova results scorecard," which links country program management and resource allocation.

The Bank has improved its approach to managing and monitoring global programs and partnerships. The Bank now has more robust systems to track involvement in global programs and partnerships, thus encouraging selectivity and quality at entry. All programs receiving Development Grant Facility funding of $300,000 or more, over the life of the program, are also subject to independent program-level evaluations. But an IEG assessment of a cross-section of such evaluations found their quality frequently compromised by weak M&E systems, particularly a lack of systematic evidence on the achievement of programs' objectives at the outcome level. Therefore, it is difficult to say whether the global programs reviewed—together accounting for about $100 million of annual spending—ultimately had a substantial effect on the ground.

Two recent developments may hold promise for the Bank's results agenda, although they are in their early days. The first is the use of impact evaluations: the number supported by the Bank has more than doubled, to 158 over the past year. Impact evaluations are not a panacea but can create better understanding of the causal links and factors contributing to the outcomes of projects, programs, and policies. However, these evaluations are concentrated in a few areas (education, health, and conditional cash transfers) and need to be managed more strategically to draw more knowledge from them.

The second development is a new approach toward measuring and reporting on development results for the International Development Association (IDA)— the Bank's main source of concessional finance. The results management system for IDA—initiated in the 14th replenishment of IDA, with commitments to enhance it in the 15th replenishment (IDA15)—tries, among other things, to spotlight changes in indicators, including access to water and measures of child health. It is premature to assess how well this will work, but it is an important step in corporate-level monitoring and evaluation. At the same time, there are difficult questions as to whether and how a more comprehensive results framework for the Bank, as a whole, could evolve. It continues to be difficult to piece together the various M&E indicators to form a view of the Bank's overall development results.

There are two broad lessons for better tracking Bank performance. First, practical steps are needed (a) at the project level, and in global and regional programs, to enhance the quality of the M&E systems, especially by working to put in place good baseline information and to elucidate clearly the link between project outputs and targeted outcomes; (b) at the country level, to simplify results frameworks and so make them more useful in guiding and evaluating programs; and (c) at the institutional level, for the Bank and in partner countries, to manage and learn from a growing number of impact evaluations, including by better integrating them into country programs and exploiting cross-country synergies in conducting and sharing studies. Second, the Bank and IEG should strengthen the evaluation knowledge base for the Bank's corporate results. Progress on these two fronts will improve the prospects for greater development impact in the years ahead.

Part II: Shared Global Challenges

The Challenge of Global Public Goods

Tackling global climate change and providing other important global public goods present some of the greatest challenges of our time. Indeed, many global public goods are chronically undersupplied. Why? Because it is difficult to secure collective action among nations to provide a public good—such as keeping air clean—particularly when the costs are borne locally while the benefits are largely captured nationally or globally. Yet there is a growing interconnection between the different types of investments and actions needed at various levels to foster global public goods.

The World Bank Group has emphasized the need to foster global public goods as one of its main priorities in the future. The effective provision of global public goods increasingly influences development results (discussed in Part I above), especially addressing the many dimensions of poverty, including vulnerability. The Bank's strategic framework for its role with regard to global public goods notes that the Bank can connect global concerns to country programs and advocate for collective international action. How can the Bank enhance its effectiveness in this area?

Can the Bank's Country-Based Model Foster Global Public Goods?

Relying on the country-based model as the platform for the Bank's work on global public goods is a double-edged sword. The model works well when national partners see an alignment between domestic and global benefits, and when the Bank has an attractive instrument to help implement action at the country level. For example, the Bank's successful work in client countries, to help phase out ozone-depleting substances, benefited from the existence of the Montreal Protocol—a binding agreement that committed countries to globally agreed action—and the Multilateral Fund, which provided resources for investments. Global Environment Facility (GEF) grants have also been well integrated into Bank country programs, such as in China, where a large GEF portfolio has buttressed growing attention to environmental issues. And in Vietnam, the Bank has been able to use its multisectoral expertise, combined with concessional finance, to help the authorities cope with the threat of avian flu, in part because there was strong national interest in averting economic fallout in the domestic food industry.

The country-based model, however, comes under strain, especially when global and country interests are seen to diverge significantly and the Bank's traditional tools, including its lending, do not gain traction with clients. This makes it doubly difficult to secure progress with global public goods. Tackling climate change requires huge adjustments in various economic behaviors, including reducing emissions and improving economywide energy efficiency and use. For many countries, the benefits of such actions seem remote while the costs accrue in the near term. To date, though, the Bank has not been able to call on an attractive large-scale funding program or invoke an international framework to encourage comprehensive action on climate change. It will be important to see how the recently discussed Climate Investment Funds help improve this situation.

The Bank pays attention to fostering global public goods in its high-level corporate strategies and the topic has been emphasized by the president as one of the Bank's six strategic pillars. However, attention wanes as one moves down the levels from corporate strategies to sectoral or regional strategies, and then down one more level to country strategies. Both the Bank's *GPG Framework* and *Long-Term Strategic Exercise* discussed global public goods extensively but lacked specifics on how to translate corporate priorities into country action. The treatment in strategies at the next level down—the Bank's networks and Regional units—varies significantly. Attention to global public goods is more prominent in both sectoral and Regional strategies dealing with the environment than in those dealing with the health sector. This may be due to the type of intervention needed in health sector global public goods—such as communicable disease control, which requires a strong national focus that might not be explicitly connected to global action.

The systems for integrating global public goods into country strategies are underdeveloped. Environmental commons is frequently noted in country strategies (in part because GEF projects are mainstreamed in the Bank's systems), but other global public goods are less often emphasized. There is no evidence that over time the treatment of global public goods in Bank country strategies has expanded, but very recent examples of good practice—such as in Brazil—may pave the way for more thorough and consistent strategic planning.

The Bank has at least three levers for moving from strategy to action at the country level—budget and trust fund allocation, financing instruments, and global programs. Each is discussed in turn below.

RESOURCE ALLOCATION

The Bank estimates its administrative expenditure on global public goods at around $110 million in fiscal 2007, nearly half of which is from sources that are outside the Bank's core budget, such as trust funds. At about 4 percent of its overall operating budget, this is one of the smaller allocations for the Bank's six strategic priorities. These estimates should be treated with some caution because they may vary significantly, depending on the definitions and data classifications used. Going forward, a more precise definition and tracking of spending on global public goods would be a useful management tool.

A heavy reliance on trust funds for financing global public goods work may itself increase the difficulties of mainstreaming such activity alongside long-standing work financed by the Bank's own budget. Spending on global public goods, as a whole, has risen rapidly over the past five years, with the biggest increase for work on environmental commons.

FINANCING INSTRUMENTS

Concessional finance is important to foster many global public goods, and in recent years, the Bank has committed substantial IDA funding to help countries in programs with clear global public goods dimensions, such as HIV/AIDS and environmental commons. Often, country-level implementation capacity is stretched, however, and national priorities may take precedence over some global public goods considerations. Staff report that there is great reluctance among national partners and Bank country teams to allow IDA allocations targeted for poverty reduction to be diverted to fostering global public goods, which may not immediately benefit the poorest populations. A recent innovation in IDA is a specific allocation for regional (multicountry) projects. Although it is too early to assess how well this is working, it should be monitored for lessons in mirroring this approach for some global public goods; great care would be needed to avoid fragmenting IDA's overall framework.

When the Bank has had a clear and viable instrument to help its country partners take action on some global public goods, there has been progress—the GEF is a good example. Where the Bank has not had an obviously attractive financial instrument—and/or where there has been a lack of demand from country partners—it is less easy to see progress. Measures to protect and conserve important forest resources around the world, for example, have produced a highly varied picture. In Indonesia, an evaluation of the Bank's country assistance program from 1999 to 2006 showed that it covered forestry issues with large-scale analytical work but little lending. Over that period, the traction achieved by the Bank was very limited, and deforestation continued at a rapid clip.

There is often a mismatch between country needs (and resources) and global ambitions for global public goods. In middle-income countries, the Bank's ability to influence (or persuade) a country to take concrete action on some global public goods is inherently limited, even though effective provision of those goods requires deep participation by these middle-income countries. The limits of nonconcessional finance are clear, for example, in the Bank's work on avian influenza, where only 7 of the 50 projects approved are financed by the International Bank for Reconstruction and Development (IBRD), and, to date, only $12 million of the $94 million in IBRD loans have been disbursed.

GLOBAL PROGRAMS

The Bank is now a partner in some 160 global programs and partnerships, and about 90 percent of the total spending of these global programs and partnerships, which is overseen by the Bank, is directed at global public goods. A few large initiatives account for most of this spending: the Global Fund to Fight Aids, Tuberculosis, and Malaria; the GEF; and the Consultative Group for International Agricultural Research (CGIAR). The Bank's administrative effort in global programs and partnerships is not fully driven by global public goods concerns, however, since more than 100 of these programs are focused largely on national public goods, such as urban development or regulation of the markets for infrastructure.

Despite the Bank's direct role as a partner in global programs, systematic linkages to country programs have been lacking at times. For example, many of the programs had only modest participation by middle-income countries. Task managers for global programs have not commonly been required to demonstrate how such programs have added value to country programs and Bank operations, and often lack the incentive or administrative budget to do so.

Merely locating a global program in the Bank—there are 57 such programs—does not guarantee effective country linkages. For example, linkages were weak in the Population Reproductive Health Capacity Building Program, despite the potential synergies with Bank investment operations in various countries. IEG evaluations have also found that greater legitimacy of a global program does appear to foster stronger linkages with country operations.

In the Bank's efforts to provide regional public goods—and to link regional and country concerns and opportunities—it faces challenges similar to those for global public goods. Regional programs have risen in importance in recent years, but their integration into country programs remains the exception rather than the rule, and they still account for a modest share of Bank lending.

The Bank's Advocacy on Global Public Goods: What Has Worked and What Has Not

Successful advocacy goes beyond encouraging action at the country level. It also involves producing collective global responses and promoting the development interests of the poor in international agreements and frameworks for action.

Promoting improvements in the global trading framework is an example of the Bank's advocacy at its best. Key ingredients included a long period of working directly with partner countries, the assembly of first-rate intellectual and analytical research capacity, proactive and highly visible dissemination, and the willingness to engage in public debate. These were combined to excellent effect, and the Bank's work also had an opportunity to gain traction in the context of "live" negotiations for the Doha round of a new international trade agreement.

The experience with avian flu also illustrates the Bank's strengths as an advocate and convener. The Bank's contributions to a global response was built on robust economic analysis, convening power, fiduciary reputation, and multisectoral expertise. It also helped that the ground was fertile for the Bank's advocacy, given that global and national concerns aligned as country needs were urgently felt.

Advocacy on environmental commons has proved a more complex challenge. The Bank has played a positive advocacy role in some very practical settings, including the securing of resources for the GEF, the launch of the Prototype Carbon Fund (and subsequent carbon funds), and methodologies to put the Clean Development Mechanism into action. The extent to which the Bank has been a leading influential advocate on climate change is more debatable, but there is now a platform on which to build future advocacy work, including the Bank's new Strategic Framework for Climate Change.

Advocacy through global programs has become an increasingly important channel for fostering global public goods. Giving proper voice and representation to developing countries in such programs improves their responsiveness and long-term sustainability. Yet, developing country voices remain underrepresented—not least in the governance of many global programs—and whether the Bank could have pushed harder on this issue remains a question. It is encouraging that governance arrangements in several programs, including the GEF and CGIAR, have improved over time. For large new global programs aimed at climate change, it is critical to ensure sound and equitable governance arrange-

ments that balance the interests of the key parties involved.

Improving the Bank's Support for Global Public Goods: Lessons from Experience

The Bank's country model has its place in fostering global public goods. It has worked well when national and global interests coincide—often with an agreed international framework for action, such as the Montreal Protocol—and when grant finance supports country-based investments.

Looking ahead, some of the great shared global challenges arise where national and global benefits diverge significantly—most notably on climate protection. In tackling these challenges, the Bank—including through cooperation with the International Finance Corporation and Multilateral Investment Guarantee Agency—needs to find a way to bridge the gap more effectively between global needs and country preferences. Lessons from this review suggest some measures in five areas that may help the Bank upgrade its ability to foster global public goods.

First, the Bank can create better incentives to deliver global public goods effectively at the country level. This would include new approaches to setting budgets and recognizing the performance of managers and staff. On budget setting, one option is to set aside, at the corporate level, significant administrative funding to be allocated to country teams—transparently and possibly competitively—for high-priority global public goods work at the country level. Care would be needed to make sure such funding was used as a genuine addition by teams and not simply to displace other activity. To provide better incentives to staff, managers at all levels need to consider recognizing country- and global-level work on global public goods in performance management systems.

Second, the Bank can consider clearer organizational arrangements to best select, and indeed link together, responses at country, regional, and global levels. Some Regions may want to have dedicated staff advancing work on regional programs (and regional public goods), as has been done in Africa, and perhaps expand their purview to cover global public goods as well. But this is not a one-size-fits-all prescription, and other Regions may have different arrangements suitable to their circumstances.

Third, a more effective approach to the delivery of the Bank's global knowledge and capacity to country teams working on global public goods would be beneficial. To this end, the way the Bank can best deploy its expertise, particularly that of its specialists located at the center of the institution in the network anchors, should be reviewed.

Fourth, the Bank and its stakeholders could renew attention to ensuring that the perspective of developing countries is connected effectively with global responses. The Bank might be able to use its standing more powerfully to give greater voice to developing countries in the governance of significant global programs. It should take a more proactive stance in advocating for development interests—and developing country partners—in international forums (and agreements) dealing with global public goods. That would include the Bank's continuing to secure additional development assistance and promote the design and use of market-based instruments to help developing countries provide global public goods. The Bank could also explore further ways to stimulate South-South exchange of knowledge—and the development and application of new technologies designed with and for the South—to contribute to global public goods, such as climate-friendly energy production and use.

Finally, a firmer and more precise justification is needed for the costs and benefits of actions being proposed for the Bank's work on fostering global public goods, to ensure that such work is financially and institutionally sustainable over the long term. Particularly for global programs, the Bank must redouble its efforts to be more selective in its engagement and more forthright in its exiting programs whose benefits and cost-effectiveness are questionable. The Bank should also be insistent about putting in place, and using, sound results frameworks, underpinned by realistic and cost-effective monitoring and evaluation systems.

Management Comments: Summary

The 2008 *Annual Review of Development Effectiveness* (ARDE) tracks Bank performance and examines a particular thematic topic, the Bank's work in fostering global public goods (GPGs). Management values the review of project and program outcomes and of monitoring and evaluation (M&E) practice, and we appreciate in particular the clarity of analysis, which helps the Bank learn from experience.

We very much welcome also the review of country program support for GPGs and of the Bank's advocacy work on GPGs, particularly the recommendations on bridging the gap between global needs and country preferences. Management's complete comments are included as an appendix; this note summarizes the main points, with a focus on recent actions.

Tracking Bank Performance

Project Outcomes. The ARDE confirms that project outcomes have significantly improved over the medium term, exceeding the Bank's performance benchmarks in fiscal 2004–06. Management notes with particular satisfaction impressive improvements in the projects of the Africa Region and of the water supply and sanitation sector. Management shares IEG's concerns about the dip in project outcomes in fiscal 2007, notably in noninfrastructure sectors and low-income countries, and appreciates the need to be vigilant so the dip does not become a trend. Overoptimism in self-ratings of operations close to closure parallels findings in our more detailed review of International Development Association (IDA) controls, reports by the Bank's internal Quality Assurance Group (QAG), and the India Detailed Implementation Review. In response, Bank Regions are reviewing their portfolios and working actively with staff on measures to improve rating practices and strengthen ongoing operations. A more fundamental issue, however, is that the traditional supervision model, which was geared to infrastructure projects in middle-income countries, needs to be adapted to the circumstances of projects in softer sectors and in fragile states, which call for more Bank engagement in project implementation, better risk reporting, and customized implementation support directed at capacity building. Management is addressing this issue in the context of investment lending reform.

Country Program Outcomes. The ARDE reports that outcome ratings, averaged over a long period, are considerably lower for Bank-supported programs in low-income countries (LICs) than for programs in middle-income countries (MICs), and are lower for programs than for projects. Management is concerned about the gap between MIC and LIC programs and would very much welcome IEG's deeper analysis of the underlying factors—notably an analysis of changes in outcomes over time for subgroups of countries, taking into account such developments as the introduction of Country Assistance Strategy (CAS) results frameworks and changes in evaluation methodology. Management believes that the gap between program and project outcomes primarily reflects a difference in performance standards, not a failure of programs to exploit synergies. The Bank only recently introduced results-based CASs that clearly distinguish between the country's objectives and CAS outcomes based on those objectives, and include results chains setting out how the Bank will contribute to those outcomes. Most of the programs evaluated by IEG are on based on CASs in which this distinction was much less clear. The upcoming CAS Retrospective will provide a further opportunity for an informed discussion of program outcomes.

Monitoring and Evaluation. Management agrees with the ARDE's finding that the implementation of the Bank's strong policy framework for M&E continues to face challenges in projects and programs. Management appreciates and is acting on IEG's recommendations to focus on the provision of good baseline information, articulate more clearly the link between project outputs and targeted outcomes, simplify CAS results frameworks, and use M&E more effectively for program management. To do this effectively will require not only Bank action but measures to address the issue of statistical capacity in member countries. As announced during the High-Level Forum on Aid Effectiveness in Accra, our joint efforts with the Netherlands and the United Kingdom have succeeded in establishing a new Statistics for Results Facility that will help countries implement their national plans for improving statistical systems.

Shared Global Challenges— Lessons from the Bank's Experience

Bank Support at the Country Level. The ARDE observes that GPGs other than environmental commons are not sufficiently emphasized in CASs and that the extent of Bank involvement in GPG issues varies widely among countries.

Management agrees that country-based support for GPGs will need to increase and be better integrated into CASs. We also believe that the appropriate role for the Bank is specific to the particular GPG being supported and to the country context; hence variations in the extent of Bank involvement among GPGs and among countries are to be expected. Since the Bank is only one player among many, our framework for support to GPGs calls for identifying where gaps are not being met by other agencies and then helping to fill the gaps where the Bank has the capability and comparative advantage. Country ownership and response to client demand remain the primary principles of country-based support for GPGs.

The Country Program Model. The ARDE highlights the challenges to country-based support for GPGs in cases where global and country interests diverge and there is no international framework for collective action. Management believes that such challenges can be addressed without earmarked funding at the corporate level for country work. We do not agree with the broad conclusion that relying on the country program model is a "double-edged sword." The Bank's ultimate clients are poor people. By using the country program model, the Bank is better able to provide analysis that puts growth and poverty reduction at the core and relates GPG challenges to this goal, and to ensure that the actions it supports are owned by the country. In Management's view, the key challenge—discussed in the upcoming CAS Retrospective—is to more thoroughly integrate GPGs into the CAS diagnosis of country development challenges and the dialogue with the government, and on that basis determine the appropriate contribution of global programs and trust funds as part of the CAS support program. We also agree that mobilizing concessional funding is important for engagement on GPGs in MICs, and we note that efforts to that effect are under way.

Chairperson's Summary: Committee on Development Effectiveness (CODE)

O
n July 23, 2008, the Committee on Development Effectiveness met to consider the *Annual Review of Development Effectiveness 2008: Shared Global Challenges* (ARDE), prepared by the Independent Evaluation Group (IEG), and Draft Management Comments.

2008 ARDE

Part I of the report tracked the Bank's performance (including trends in outcomes of projects and country programs), the evolution of monitoring and evaluation (M&E), and the role of evaluation in the results agenda. IEG found that overall development outcomes of Bank lending have improved over the medium term, albeit not over the past year. Noting the growing "disconnect" between project supervision ratings and final project outcome ratings (which could point to weak incentives for accurate project reporting), IEG cautioned against overoptimism in assessing ongoing project performance, and called for vigilance to ensure that the drop in project performance in fiscal 2007 does not foreshadow a persistent decline. IEG also noted opportunities to strengthen M&E.

Part II focused on a special theme, which this year was the Bank's work in fostering global public goods (GPGs). IEG found that the country-based model worked well when national and global interests coincided and when grant finance supports country-level investment, but the greatest challenges arise when actual or perceived local, national, and global benefits diverge significantly. IEG drew lessons for the Bank's consideration: (i) strengthen incentives to deliver GPGs at the country level; (ii) consider clearer organizational arrangements to best select and link responses at country, regional, and global levels; (iii) enhance the delivery of global knowledge and capacity to country teams working on GPGs; (iv) ensure that the perspectives of developing countries are effectively connected with global responses; and (v) improve the justifications for the costs and benefits of actions being proposed to foster GPGs.

Draft Management Response

Management welcomed the insightful review and agreed that vigilance is warranted with respect to the weakening development outcomes of exiting projects and the increasing "disconnect" between the Bank's self-ratings of project performance and IEG's final ratings of development outcomes in fiscal 2007. In this regard, it noted that a deeper analysis of contributing factors, especially of differences among regions and sectors, would have been useful. Management commented on the need to address the different outcomes of middle-income country (MIC) and low-income country (LIC) programs, and the issue of lower outcome ratings for country programs than for projects. It had some different views about the obstacles to better M&E. Management also offered its perspectives on efforts to integrate GPGs at the sector, country, and regional levels; its role in mobilizing and providing innovative financing; support for different types of global programs and partnerships; the proposal to set aside administrative funds to support high-priority GPGs at the country level; and the Bank's role in advocating the climate change agenda.

Overall Conclusions

The Committee heard that management found the structure and analytical context of the report to be of high quality and was broadly comfortable with the findings, with one exception regarding the recommendation to set aside earmarked country program budget for GPGs. This issue and, more broadly, the matter of the appropriate business model and incentives for integrating global and more traditional, local development interests elicited comments from most speakers, who expressed a diversity of views and also made suggestions. Another area that resonated with most participants was the "disconnect" between staff self-ratings and IEG's final ratings after project completion, which was higher in fiscal 2007 than in recent years.

The Committee appreciated management's focus on: (i) the differentials between country groupings or sectors with the aim of strengthening Bank business in dealing with the challenges of low-capacity countries and softer sectors; (ii) the findings related to low-income country programs, especially since IEG did not rate the overall development outcome of a single program beyond moderately satisfactory during the evaluation period; (iii) the distinction between project complexity and development risks related to challenging country circumstances; (iv) the emphasis on M&E not only to ensure data availability for assessing results (and avoiding complacency) but also to obtain a clearer perspective on the complementarities and tradeoffs between public goods and more traditional economic growth and development concerns; and (v) the new structure of the ARDE.

With respect to Part II on GPGs, in addition to ways of striking the appropriate balances in country programs and operations, the discussion also drew attention to several findings of corporate relevance, namely the advocacy role where the Bank must push harder to strengthen the developing countries' perspectives and voices, which are presently underrepresented. To this end, it was noted that GPGs are relatively new in the development agenda, and the Bank is at the beginning of its learning curve in assisting countries to address GPG issues. Therefore, the Committee should keep an open mind about the challenges of GPGs and avoid reaching premature conclusions.

Next Steps

The Board is scheduled to consider the report on September 9, 2008. IEG will provide a summary of actions to which management committed, in response to IEG recommendations and where IEG has seen limited progress after three years. For future ARDE reports, IEG was asked to consider a closer link between Parts I and II. Management noted that M&E and results management in country programs will be discussed under the upcoming Country Assistance Strategy (CAS) Retrospective Report.

Main issues raised at the meeting were the following:

Project Performance. Members agreed that vigilance is needed to identify problem projects and risks in real time, an issue previously raised by the Quality Assurance Group (QAG). They took note of management's recognition that the current supervision for large infrastructure projects does not differentiate between countries (low-income vs. middle-income countries and fragile situations) and between hard (infrastructure) and softer sectors (human development or public sector management). Some members acknowledged the higher fiscal 2007 "disconnect" between the Bank's self-rating of project performance and IEG's final ratings of development outcomes. They sought further comments on the cause of this "disconnect." One member suggested that the Bank and IEG should find a mutually agreed scheme; IEG noted that the rating systems were comparable.

This member also recommended that the CAS Progress Report should address the issue of quality of supervision.

Issues were raised relating to project complexity and development risks under challenging country circumstances. A point was made that project complexity should be commensurate with implementation capacity. Speakers cautioned against messages or incentives that may induce staff to avoid risks necessary to achieve development impact. One member noted that (i) for measuring complex projects, there was a question about how to integrate a risk premium into the rating system, to ensure quality but without undermining the risk-taking incentives to staff; (ii) innovative approaches were needed to address development issues in difficult countries, and (iii) the challenge was in designing interventions adapted to different categories of countries (for example, LICs, MICs, or fragile states).

Country Programs. One member noted, with concern, IEG's finding that not a single program concentrated in smaller countries or countries with extensive poverty has been rated "satisfactory" in meeting their stated development objectives. Given the long engagement of the Bank with LICs, the question arose about whether there are some systemic issues and whether these have been suitably identified.

M&E and Results Management. Members suggested that the use of impact evaluation, though still at an early stage, could improve understanding of the outcomes of projects, programs, and policies. The importance of disseminating the methodologies of impact evaluation was noted. One member observed that the quality of M&E was associated with the quality of outcomes, and expressed concern that while measuring intermediate and final outputs require appropriate data gathering, these activities were not built into project design. While acknowledging that results on the ground and success may be hard to attribute to interventions by the Bank, he questioned how it can be a knowledge bank if it cannot learn from its successes and failures. This member

further suggested that Implementation Completion Reports should include a formal requirement to rate a project's M&E. Questions were raised more generally on the quality of M&E, simplification of country results framework, and knowledge base of corporate results.

Challenge of GPGs. Members generally agreed that GPGs were a relatively new topic in the development agenda, and the Bank needed to gain experience about what may work well, including enhancement of country ownership and the demand-driven approach, as well as strengthened partnerships. They also stressed the need to identify the Bank's comparative advantage in the GPG work, given that the Bank was only one of many players in this field. One member was disappointed about the perception that "networks are not working." Some members encouraged the identification of sectoral comparative advantages beyond health and climate change, such as market stabilization of key commodities like oil and grains, and the development of innovative financing. If GPGs are in conflict with a country's interest, there is a question of ownership, incentives, and perception of tradeoffs between GPGs and development. In this sense, one member felt the Bank was focusing on "rounding a square." This member also felt that it was difficult to operationalize IEG's recommendations to improve the Bank's support for GPGs.

GPG Country-Based Model. Members felt that the country-based model was a clear comparative advantage of the Bank's work on GPGs. However, they regretted that systems for integrating GPGs into the country-based model were underdeveloped when country and global interests diverge significantly. In this context, some members underscored the importance of addressing the limitations of the current business model to promote GPGs, while avoiding imposing conditionalities and supply-driven approaches. There was a sentiment that the country-based model was not enough to address GPGs and should be complemented with a global-level framework, which will provide incentives to countries, including financial mechanisms for incremental costs. In addition, a question was raised about whether the issue was the effectiveness of Bank instruments rather than the country model.

Resource Allocation for GPGs. There were comments on the need for a new approach in allocating and tracking spending on GPGs (both budget and trust funds), and in recognizing performance, but there were a variety of views as to how this should be done. One member shared management's reservation about IEG's suggested option of setting aside significant administrative funding for allocation of high-priority GPG work at the country level.

ARDE Format. The new structure of the report generally found favor with the Committee.

Speakers welcomed the new format but would have liked greater substantive integration of the two parts. A more specific suggestion was to deepen the analysis of several key points in Part I, to make the report a more robust instrument of management's accountability. One member found that the aggregate view of the Bank's development effectiveness did not give an indication of how various areas of the Bank perform, what lessons could be drawn from the report, and thus how resources should be allocated. A few members sought clarification on why the report was not accompanied by the Management Action Record for monitoring progress of the Bank's agreed actions. IEG provided additional information regarding the implementation report that sets out which older IEG recommendations will be retired from formal consideration.

Jiayi Zou, Chairperson

Evaluation Snapshot in Selected Languages

The key findings and recommendations of the *Annual Review of Development Effectiveness 2008: Shared Global Challenges* are presented in snapshot below. Translations of the report's full summary into each of the languages shown here are available at www.worldbank.org/ieg, and hard copies are available from IEG and World Bank Public Information Centers.

Arabic عـربي

- تخفيض أعداد الفقراء في أي بلد منفرد يتشابك بصورة مطردة مع تحقيق تقدم في التصدي للتحديات العالمية المشتركة- أي تشجيع إيجاد السلع العامة العالمية مثل حماية المناخ والحد من الأمراض المعدية. ويرصد تقرير الاستعراض السنوي للفعالية الإنمائية لهذه السنة أداء البنك الدولي في الجزء الأول ويبحث عمل البنك في مجال تشجيع إيجاد السلع العامة العالمية في الجزء الثاني.

- تحسنت نواتج التنمية من إقراض البنك في الأمد المتوسط. ولكن في السنة المالية ٢٠٠٧ ارتفع بشدة مستوى الإفراط في التفاؤل في تقييم البنك المستمر لأداء المشروعات، بينما انخفضت نسبة المشروعات التي قيمت باعتبارها مرضية بدرجة معتدلة أو أفضل إلى ٧٦ في المائة مقابل ٨٣ في المائة في السنة السابقة.

- يحتاج الأمر إلى اليقظة لتحديد المشروعات التي تعاني من مشاكل في التو واللحظة والتأكد من أن الهبوط في مستوى الأداء في السنة المالية ٢٠٠٧ لا ينذر بهبوط مستمر. ويمكن اتخاذ خطوات عملية لتحسين استخدام المتابعة والتقييم في المشروعات والبرامج، بما في ذلك توفير معلومات أساسية سليمة وزيادة وضوح الصلات بين النتائج والنواتج.

- يعمل النموذج القطري للبنك بصورة جيدة نسبيا في تشجيع إيجاد السلع العامة العالمية عندما تتسق المصالح الوطنية والعالمية وعندما تساند المنح الاستثمارات القطرية. غير أن أعظم التحديات، مثل تغير المناخ، تنشأ عندما تتباين بشدة المنافع المحلية والوطنية والعالمية – الفعلية أو المتصورة. وهنا يتعرض هذا النموذج القطري لضغوط كبيرة.

- لسد الفجوة بين الاحتياجات العالمية والاهتمامات القطرية بصورة أكثر فعالية، يتعين على البنك بحث: وضع موازنات مخصصة وحوافز أفضل للفرق القطرية للعمل على إيجاد السلع العامة العالمية؛ وتحسين نشر شبكات معارف العالمية؛ واستخدام مركزه بصورة أقوى لمنح صوت أكبر للبلدان النامية في نظام إدارة البرامج العالمية.

Chinese 中文

- 在单个国家减少贫困的工作日益与解决全球共同挑战（即促进气候保护和传染病控制等全球公共产品的生产）的进展相互关联。今年的 ARDE 第一部分论述了世界银行的绩效，第二部分总结了世行在促进全球公共产品方面的工作。

- 从中期来看，世行贷款的发展效益有所提高。但在 2007 财政年度，世行对项目绩效过分乐观的程度急剧上升。相比之下，一年前评为满意度中等或更高的项目比例从 83% 下降到 76%。

- 世行必须提高警觉度，随时查明有问题的项目，避免 2007 财政年度业绩的下降成为长期性下降趋势的先兆。世行可以采取具体步骤，在项目和方案中加强监督和评估工作，包括收集正确的基线信息，明确产出与成果之间的关系。

- 当国家的利益和全球利益相辅相成、赠款能够对国家的投资产生支持作用时，世行的国别工作模型在促进全球公共产品生产方面达到了较好的效果。然而，当地方、国家和全球利益（包括实际存在的利益和人们想象中的利益）存在重大差异时，气候变化等问题就成为极其严重的挑战。在这种情况下，国别工作模型受到了巨大压力。

- 为了更有效地填补解决全球需求与解决国家需求之间的差距，世行应考虑采取以下措施：建立专用预算和改进鼓励措施，促使国别团队为全球公共产品而工作；增强对全球知识网络的利用；进一步利用世行的重要地位在全球方案治理方面增加发展中国家的发言权。

English	French	Français

- Reducing poverty in any individual country is increasingly intertwined with making progress on shared global challenges—that is, fostering global public goods (GPGs) such as climate protection and communicable disease control. This year's ARDE tracks World Bank performance in Part I and examines the Bank's work in fostering GPGs in Part II.

- Development outcomes from Bank lending have improved over the medium term. But in fiscal 2007 overoptimism in the Bank's ongoing assessment of project performance rose sharply, while the share of projects rated moderately satisfactory or better dropped to 76 percent from 83 percent a year earlier.

- Vigilance is needed to identify problem projects in real time and ensure that the fiscal 2007 drop in performance does not foreshadow a persistent decline. Practical steps can be taken to better use M&E in projects and programs, including proper baseline information and clearer links between outputs and outcomes.

- The Bank's country-based model has worked relatively well in fostering global public goods when national and global interests dovetail and grants support country investments. But the greatest challenges, such as climate change, arise where local, national, and global benefits—actual or perceived—diverge significantly. Here the country model comes under considerable strain.

- To more effectively bridge the gap between global needs and country concerns, the Bank should consider: creating dedicated budgets and better incentives for country teams to work on GPGs; deploying its global knowledge networks better; and using its standing more powerfully to give greater voice to developing countries in the governance of global programs.

- Dans chaque pays, la réduction de la pauvreté est de plus en plus étroitement liée aux progrès réalisés face aux grands problèmes communs à l'ensemble de la planète – autrement dit, à la promotion des biens publics mondiaux, tels que la protection du climat et la lutte contre les maladies communicables. Cette année, l'Examen annuel de l'efficacité du développement consacre sa Première partie à suivre les résultats obtenus par la Banque mondiale dans ce domaine et sa Deuxième partie à l'action menée par la Banque pour promouvoir les biens publics mondiaux.

- Un bilan des résultats obtenus par les prêts de la Banque laisse apparaître une amélioration sur le moyen terme. Toutefois, au cours de l'exercice 2007, l'excès d'optimisme affiché par la Banque dans son évaluation de la performance de ses projets a grimpé fortement alors même que le pourcentage de ses projets classés comme modérément satisfaisants ou mieux est tombé à 76% contre 83% l'année précédente.

- Il faut faire preuve de vigilance si l'on veut identifier les projets à problème en temps réel et veiller à ce que la baisse de résultats de 2007 ne soit pas annonciatrice d'un déclin persistant. On peut prendre des mesures pratiques afin de mieux utiliser le Suivi et l'Évaluation dans les projets et programmes, notamment une bonne information de base et des liens clairement établis entre les produits et les résultats.

- Le modèle par pays de la Banque contribue assez efficacement à promouvoir les biens publics mondiaux lorsque les intérêts nationaux concordent avec les intérêts mondiaux et que des dons soutiennent les investissements du pays. En revanche, les problèmes les plus graves, tels que le changement climatique, se posent lorsque les intérêts nationaux et mondiaux – réels ou perçus – divergent sensiblement. En pareil cas, le modèle par pays est mis à rude épreuve.

- Pour mieux combler le fossé entre les besoins mondiaux et les préoccupations nationales, la Banque devrait envisager : d'établir des budgets spécifiques et de meilleures incitations pour les équipes-pays à travailler à la réalisation des biens publics mondiaux ; de mieux utiliser ses réseaux mondiaux de savoir ; et d'utiliser plus énergiquement sa position afin de donner plus de voix aux pays en développement dans la gestion des programmes mondiaux.

Portuguese — Português

- A redução da pobreza em qualquer país está cada vez mais vinculada ao progresso em enfrentar desafios globais compartilhados – ou seja, promover os bens públicos globais (GPGs), tais como proteção climática e controle de doenças transmissíveis. A Revisão Anual da Eficácia do Desenvolvimento (ARDE) deste ano analisa o desempenho do Banco Mundial na Parte I e o trabalho do mesmo na promoção dos GPGs na Parte II.
- Os resultados do desenvolvimento oriundos da concessão de empréstimos pelo Banco Mundial melhoraram no médio prazo. Mas no exercício financeiro de 2007 o superotimismo da avaliação contínua do Banco Mundial no tocante ao desempenho dos projetos aumentou consideravelmente, ao passo que a parcela de projetos classificados como moderadamente satisfatórios ou melhores caiu para 76% com relação a 83% do ano anterior.
- É preciso vigilância para identificar projetos problemáticos em tempo real e assegurar que a queda de desempenho ocorrida no exercício financeiro de 2007 não seja um prenúncio de um declínio persistente. Podem-se tomar medidas para melhorar o uso de Monitoramento e Avaliação (M&A) em projetos e programas, inclusive informação básica adequada e vínculos mais claros entre produtos e resultados.
- O modelo baseado no país, utilizado pelo Banco Mundial, tem funcionado relativamente bem na promoção dos bens públicos globais em uma época em que os interesses nacionais e globais se concatenam e subvenções apóiam investimentos dos países. No entanto, os maiores desafios, tais como a mudança climática, surgem quando os benefícios locais, nacionais e globais – reais ou percebidos – divergem de forma significativa. Neste aspecto o modelo de país sofre pressão considerável.
- Para cobrir com mais eficácia o hiato entre as necessidades globais e as preocupações dos países, o Banco Mundial deve considerar mudanças tais como: Criar orçamentos dedicados e maiores incentivos para as equipes de país trabalharem na promoção dos GPGs; melhorar a implantação de suas redes globais de conhecimentos; e utilizar sua posição de forma mais incisiva para dar maior expressão aos países em desenvolvimento na governabilidade de programas globais.

Spanish — Español

- La reducción de la pobreza en un país determinado está cada vez más relacionada con los progresos que se hagan con respecto a los desafíos mundiales comunes, es decir, la promoción de los bienes públicos mundiales (BPM), como la protección del clima y la lucha contra las enfermedades transmisibles. En la Parte I de la versión del ARDE de este año se hace un seguimiento del desempeño del Banco Mundial y en la Parte II se pasa revista a su labor de promoción de los BPM.
- Los resultados en términos de desarrollo de las operaciones de financiamiento del Banco han mejorado en el mediano plazo. Sin embargo, en el ejercicio de 2007, el exceso de optimismo de las autoevaluaciones en curso con respecto al desempeño de los proyectos aumentó marcadamente, mientras que la proporción de proyectos que recibieron una calificación de moderadamente satisfactorios o superior bajó al 76%, en comparación con el 83% en el ejercicio anterior.
- Se debe prestar atención para detectar de inmediato los proyectos que presentan problemas y velar por que la baja registrada en el ejercicio de 2007 no sea un presagio de un deterioro persistente. Se pueden tomar medidas prácticas para utilizar de mejor manera los sistemas de seguimiento y evaluación en los proyectos y programas, como recopilar información básica adecuada y definir más claramente los vínculos entre los productos y los efectos directos.
- El modelo del Banco centrado en los países ha funcionado relativamente bien para promover los BPM cuando se han conjugado los intereses nacionales y de alcance mundial y las inversiones en los países se han respaldado con donaciones. Sin embargo, los mayores desafíos se plantean cuando los beneficios locales, nacionales y mundiales —ya sean reales o percibidos— difieren considerablemente. En esos casos, el modelo se debilita de manera significativa.
- Para salvar de manera más eficaz la brecha entre las necesidades de alcance mundial y los temas que interesan a los países, el Banco debería contemplar la posibilidad de establecer presupuestos especiales y ofrecer mejores incentivos para que los equipos a cargo de las operaciones del Banco en los países se dediquen a los PBM; utilizar sus redes de conocimientos mundiales de manera más eficaz, y aprovechar de manera más enérgica su posición para dar mayor voz a los países en desarrollo en la gestión de los programas mundiales.

Russian   **Русский**

- Сокращение бедности в любой отдельной стране все чаще оказывается в зависимости от прогресса в решении общих глобальных задач, т.е. от содействия созданию глобальных общественных благ (ГОБ), таких как защита климата Земли и предотвращение распространения инфекционных заболеваний. В Части I ГОЭР за этот год рассматривается эффективность деятельности Всемирного банка, а в Части II – работа Банка, направленная на содействие созданию ГОБ.

- Результаты в области развития, связанные с кредитной деятельностью Банка, улучшились в среднесрочной перспективе. Однако 2007 год был отмечен существенным излишним оптимизмом при проведении Банком самооценок эффективности осуществляемых проектов, в то время как доля проектов, оцененных как умеренно удовлетворительные и лучше, уменьшилась с почти 83 процентов в 2006 финансовом году до 76 процентов в 2007 финансовом году.

- Для выявления проблемных проектов в режиме реального времени необходимо проявлять бдительность, чтобы не оказалось, что за наметившимся в 2007 году ухудшением показателей кроется устойчивый спад. Можно принять практические меры, направленные на более эффективное использование систем МИО на уровне проектов и программ, включая обеспечение надежной базисной информации и более четкое определение взаимосвязи между результатами проектов и целевыми достижениями.

- Модель Банка, основанная на страновом подходе, относительно эффективно работает в плане содействия созданию глобальных общественных благ, когда пересекаются национальные и глобальные интересы и когда инвестиции в странах поддерживаются грантовым финансированием. Однако наиболее трудные задачи, в том числе в сфере изменения климата, встают в тех случаях, когда местные, национальные и глобальные блага – реальные или подразумеваемые, – существенно расходятся между собой. В этом случае модель, основанная на страновом подходе, подвергается значительному давлению.

- Для того чтобы более эффективно перекрыть разрыв между глобальными потребностями и тем, что беспокоит отдельные страны, Банку следует рассмотреть возможность введения целевых бюджетов и более эффективных стимулов для страновых групп при ведении работы в отношении ГОБ; более эффективного применения глобальных систем знаний; и более действенного использования его положения с целью придать больший голос развивающимся странам в управлении глобальными программами.

Chapter 1

Evaluation Highlights

- Development success in any individual country is increasingly intertwined with making progress on shared global challenges.
- The *Annual Review of Development Effectiveness* is in a new, two-part format.
- Part I tracks World Bank performance by analyzing projects, country programs, and results from monitoring and evaluation.
- Part II examines a special topic: the Bank's work in fostering global public goods.

Chinese lanterns at night; photo ©Frank Krahmer/zefa/Corbis, reproduced by permission.

Introduction

For the World Bank and its partners, the ever-present test is to deliver results—to lift people out of poverty and promote socially and environmentally sustainable development. Achieving such success in any individual country is increasingly intertwined with making progress on shared global challenges. A fair and efficient international trade regime, for example, is a global public good (GPG) that allows developing countries to trade more and grow faster. The growing global threat of climate change—a "public bad" by contrast—particularly imperils the poor who bear the brunt of more frequent natural disasters and hazards to health and agriculture (IEG 2006b; Stern 2006).

This year's *Annual Review of Development Effectiveness* (ARDE) is in a new format and presents evidence on the Bank's efforts in two important and connected areas. Part I, which is a standard section of the new format, analyzes the trends in outcomes of Bank projects and country programs in recent years. Equally important—and building on past practice[1]—the report goes beyond performance indicators and digs deeper into the framework employed by the Bank to monitor and evaluate its work. This ARDE assembles the available evidence on how monitoring and evaluation (M&E) systems are progressing, both in terms of quality and coverage. It illustrates how new techniques are beginning to be employed, including impact evaluations and new results management systems for the International Development Association (IDA). The review also refers to evidence to benchmark the Independent Evaluation Group's (IEG's) own contribution to influencing the Bank's performance.

All of this is important because a successful M&E system that focuses on results can have three major benefits. It can provide an early warning when an intervention is not working well, and a basis for improving a project during implementation. It can provide a broad measure of results for accountability and demonstrate to stakeholders the degree to which the Bank has contributed to development results. Finally, it can contribute to global knowledge for development, providing useful lessons for other projects and programs within the same country, or within the same sector in other countries.

Part II of the report examines a special topic. There has been enormous growth in international attention to the great shared global challenges of our time—a set of supranational issues collectively known as *global public goods*. This year's ARDE looks at the Bank's work in fostering GPGs, such as protecting the earth's climate and preventing the spread of dangerous communicable diseases. GPGs are clearly important in their own right and are becoming ever more closely associated with the Bank's development impact (as described in Part I). To fight the many dimensions of poverty—including vulnerability—the world must be able not only to help antipoverty programs at the individual country level, but also to create the framework for collective action on transnational issues that can support or undermine the fate of the poor.

As the Bank has emphasized inclusive and sustainable globalization, the importance of coordinated global solutions to cross-border problems has risen in tandem. Indeed, the Bank has identified fostering GPGs as one of its six strategic themes. This report focuses on two roles the Bank has identified as its comparative advantage: (i) identifying how the Bank's country-based model has helped or hindered its support for GPGs, and (ii) drawing lessons from the Bank's experience as an advocate for action on GPGs.

The thematic focus of ARDE 2008, taken together with the components of Part I of the report, helps inform important choices for the Bank's strategy and its implementation. It also sets a framework for work by IEG in other evaluations—including next year's ARDE—to focus attention on development impact in the future.

PART I

Tracking Bank Performance

Chapter 2

Evaluation Highlights

- Project outcome ratings improved over the medium term.
- Attention is needed to address the growing lack of realism in assessments of ongoing project performance.
- Unsatisfactory projects in fiscal 2007 were hampered by overly ambitious objectives, complexity, and inadequate design.
- Many country programs produced satisfactory outcomes, especially those in large countries where many of the world's poor live.
- Overall, however, some 40 percent of country programs have been moderately unsatisfactory or worse in outcomes.

Tuareg child turns water pump wheel; photo ©Yann Arthus-Bertrand/Corbis,
reproduced by permission.

Development Outcomes: Indicators of Performance

O ver the past five years, the Bank's lending has risen in real terms, and IDA made record commitments of $12 billion in fiscal 2007, alongside some $13 billion of International Bank for Reconstruction and Development (IBRD) finance provided to middle-income countries (MICs). Indeed, with the successful 15th replenishment round for IDA resources ($42 billion), the Bank plans to maintain total annual lending in the $22 to $26 billion range during fiscal 2008–10.

Lending volumes by themselves, of course, are not an indicator of development impact, and there have been many cautions for the Bank (and other development agencies) to take care to avoid a "lending culture" which places undue emphasis on volumes delivered rather than outcomes secured.[1] There are indicators of performance that can tell us about the Bank's development impact—notably IEG evaluations of Bank-supported projects and country programs. Overall trends and recent developments revealed in both of these metrics are presented below.

Measuring Project Performance: Trends from IEG Monitoring

How are Bank-supported projects performing in terms of achieving their development objectives? The performance of Bank projects in delivering development results has unquestionably improved over the medium term.[2] In the three years to end-fiscal 2007, 80 percent of projects were moderately satisfactory or better in delivering their targeted results, up from around 70 percent

at the start of the decade, as shown in figure 2.1.

Lending outcomes have improved over the medium term.

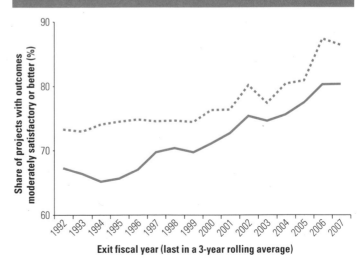

Figure 2.1: Project Performance Has Improved over the Medium Term

Share of projects with outcomes moderately satisfactory or better (%)

Exit fiscal year (last in a 3-year rolling average)

—— By number of projects   ···· Weighted by value of project disbursements
Source: World Bank database.

9

Project ratings moved up the scale in recent years.

A comparison of five-year subperiods shows 78 percent of projects from fiscal 2003 to 2007 rated as moderately satisfactory or better in achieving their development results. This is a significant improvement from fiscal 1998–2002, in which 73 percent of projects had outcomes rated moderately satisfactory or better. Illustrations of development impact from some of these projects are in box 2.1. Moreover, a growing share of projects has outcomes that are sustainable.[3] Almost 80 percent of projects evaluated in fiscal 2003–07 were rated as likely to be sustainable, up from 64 percent in the previous five years.[4] A more detailed assessment of project performance is available in appendix A.

Against the backdrop of this overall improvement in outcomes, there are several features that illustrate changes in the performance of Bank-supported projects, as shown in table 2.1. There has been a steep decline in the share of projects rated unsatisfactory while, simultaneously, the share reaching the satisfactory standard held steady. In addition, the Bank and its clients have improved a number of projects, which in the past may have been rated moderately unsatisfactory, to reach the level of moderately satisfactory. As a result, a greater proportion of projects is being rated in the middle of the scale.

Outcomes of projects in two-thirds of sectors improved, while health and public sector governance worsened.

The Bank's lending is spread across a spectrum of sectors. It is encouraging that, as shown in figure 2.2, project performance in about two-thirds of sectors has improved over the medium term.[5] The turnaround in the water supply and sanitation sector projects is especially dramatic: in fiscal 1998–2002 only a little more than 60 percent of projects (by value of disbursements) were moderately satisfactory or better, and this sector now comes close to leading the way in fiscal 2003–07, with over 90 percent of projects having moderately satisfactory or better outcomes. While there has been a creditable and significant uplift in economic policy project performance, the share of moderately satisfactory or better project outcomes in fiscal 2003–07 still trails other sectors by quite some margin. The largest declines in performance were in health, nutrition, and population (which, along with economic policy and the environment, were significantly below the Bank-wide average for the fiscal 2003–07 period) and in public sector governance.

Looking at the Regional aspects of project performance, figure 2.3 shows that the East Asia and Pacific and the Europe and Central Asia Regions led the way for the fiscal 2003–07 cohort. Their share of projects with moderately satisfactory or better outcome ratings significantly exceeded the Bank average of 83 percent (weighted by disbursement). A good illustration

---

Box 2.1: What Does a Satisfactory Project Look Like? Illustrations of Development Impact

There is no single metric that can be used across projects to assess satisfactory outcomes. Rather, development results span a range of different social and economic indicators depending on the sector and type of project. A project is rated satisfactory when the operation's objectives have been achieved with only minor shortcomings. This is illustrated with one type of development impact in Mozambique, where Bank-supported water and sanitation projects built 130 water source points, bringing drinking water to 62,000 people. And in Cambodia, a Bank-financed project brought clean water to 750,000 people in Phnom Penh.

In the energy sector, a Bank electrification project in the Lao People's Democratic Republic provided main-power-grid electricity to 51,000 households in 721 rural villages, while another 6,000 households gained access to off-grid electricity through solar and hydro systems. Having electricity greatly increased productivity of new small-scale, home-based businesses, and enabled children to study at night.

Finally, another type of development impact is demonstrated in Mali, where the Bank-supported Grassroots Initiatives to Fight Poverty and Hunger Project helped more than 6,000 children to attend school, as well as created small-scale health centers in 19 villages.

Table 2.1: Distribution of Project Ratings Moved Up the Scale in FY03–07

IEG rating of projects meeting development objectives	Percentage of Projects in Rating Category		
	FY98–02	FY03–07	Percentage point change
Highly satisfactory	6%	4%	–2
Satisfactory	45%	45%	0
Moderately satisfactory	21%	29%	+8
Moderately unsatisfactory	9%	10%	+1
Unsatisfactory	16%	10%	–6
Highly unsatisfactory	2%	1%	–1

Source: World Bank database.

of such successful performance can be seen in an agricultural development project in China's Anning Valley. The Bank's $120 million of support supplied more reliable irrigation, introduced new plant varieties and cultivation techniques, and added value to production through processing. Local farmers in the project's area enjoyed a tripling in their per capita income; the propor-

Figure 2.2: Trends in Sectoral Performance

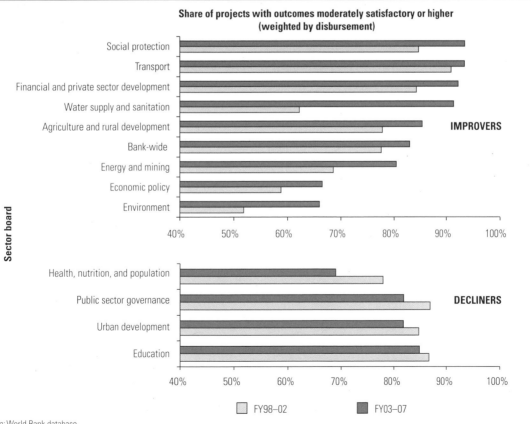

Share of projects with outcomes moderately satisfactory or higher (weighted by disbursement)

Source: World Bank database.

Note: The Sector Board classification applies to the whole project and enables outcomes to be matched to it.

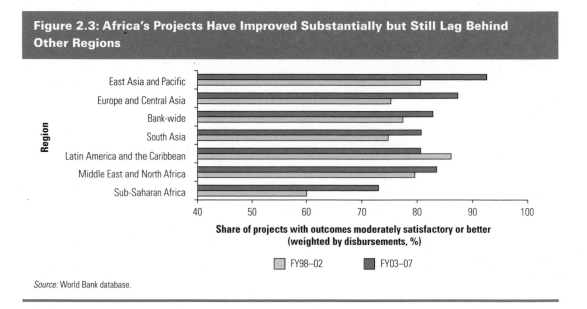

Figure 2.3: Africa's Projects Have Improved Substantially but Still Lag Behind Other Regions

Share of projects with outcomes moderately satisfactory or better
(weighted by disbursements, %)

FY98–02 FY03–07

Source: World Bank database.

tion of the area's families living in poverty fell from one-third to one-tenth; and the project generated a 27 percent rate of return on its investment.

In these Regions, MICs make up a large share of the client base, and their relatively strong institutional capacity is conducive to stronger project implementation. Nonetheless, the Bank could well be faced with increasing demands from these clients to take on projects that are complex or located within a country's lagging or remote subregions, under difficult operating conditions. These are challenges for the Bank to embrace, but expectations for the success of projects must be adjusted to recognize concomitant risks.

Africa's performance improved the most of any Region but still lags behind other parts of the Bank. In the Africa Region, the share of projects with moderately satisfactory or better outcomes improved the most of any Region over fiscal 2003–07. Again, it should be acknowledged that difficult operating conditions can make it difficult to secure success—and that may at least partly explain why project performance, overall, in Africa continues to lag behind all other Regions. But the Bank has to find ways to deliver outcomes in adversity, as a central part of its mission. Indeed, this can be done, as illustrated in the Bank's $220 million investment to assist war-affected households in

northern Ethiopia. By removing landmines, building new homes, and equipping households with basic goods and agricultural inputs—including seeds and fertilizer—some 67,000 families returned home, rebuilt their lives, and generated new economic activity, which delivered a 50 percent return on the project's investment.

Project Outcomes in Fiscal 2007 Data

Project development outcome ratings fluctuate, sometimes significantly, from year to year. Differences are sometimes a result of the vicissitudes of a particular cohort of projects rather than a substantive change in underlying institutional or partner performance. So while a single year's data should not be taken in isolation, the most recent data are worth examining to see whether any patterns or signals emerge. There are two movements in fiscal 2007 that warrant the attention of Bank management.[6]

First, increasingly the Bank is too optimistic in its own assessment of ongoing project performance. Of the 45 projects that exited in fiscal 2007 and were rated as moderately unsatisfactory or worse by IEG, over two-thirds—32 projects in total—had been reported by the Bank as moderately satisfactory or better just before they were closed. This failure to identify problem projects early impairs real-time managing for results, since overly optimistic ongoing ratings mean management is less likely to take remedial action. Most Regions were too optimistic in their ongoing reporting of project ratings for fiscal 2007, with almost a fifth of all projects—and in Africa close to a third—downgraded during the process of self-evaluation and independent evaluation.[7] Comparatively, these "disconnect" rates in previous years were much lower—less than 1 in 10 were downgraded in fiscal 2005 and 2006, as shown in table 2.2. Reducing this disconnect—by more carefully and accurately identifying underperforming projects during implementation—is needed to focus attention on project supervision and to improve performance. Of course, to subsequently improve development outcomes will then require project-specific actions on the ground.

Second, in fiscal 2007 there was a significant fall to 76 percent in the share of projects rated moderately satisfactory or better, from 83 percent in fiscal 2006.[8] This absolute level of performance still meets the 75 percent target set by the Bank a decade ago, although it is lower than the 80 percent benchmark noted by the Bank's own Quality Assurance Group (QAG) in recent annual reviews. If a 75 percent threshold for project portfolio performance is considered reasonable, given the risks of the "development business," then this one-year drop, by itself, is not too worrisome. But certainly vigilance is needed to ensure that this drop does not foreshadow a persistent decline.

What has caused the drop in ratings in fiscal 2007 and produced 45 projects with outcomes moderately unsatisfactory or worse? Sometimes a difference in the performance of the Bank's portfolio from one year to the next can be influenced by a change in the composition of projects being evaluated—for example, if there is a larger share of projects in challenging sectors or countries. But the change in portfolio composition in fiscal 2007—related to Region, sector, instrument, lending arm, and other factors—does not explain the fall in ratings. Even if the fiscal 2007 cohort had maintained the same composition of lending to conflict-affected and postconflict countries as the fiscal 2004–06 cohorts, the result would not be materially affected. Appendix A shows the impact of various changes in the fiscal 2007 composition in more detail.

Ongoing self-assessments of project performance are increasingly overly optimistic.

Another possible explanation is that the drop in measured project performance is due to methodological changes in the way projects were evaluated in fiscal 2007. Some changes in methods were introduced by IEG and the Bank together in fiscal 2007 to strengthen the robustness of project ratings and to cover new elements of project design. In the near term they may have introduced some element of discontinuity in the data series between fiscal 2007 and earlier years.[9] It is estimated that the influence of methodology changes has been small—accounting for around 1 percentage point of the fall.

Project outcomes deteriorated in fiscal 2007.

The final possibility is that in the fiscal 2007 cohort, there was simply a greater occurrence of five key factors influencing weak outcomes. First, poor or overly complex project design has been a problem in more than half of these underper-

Table 2.2: Disconnect between the Bank's Self-Ratings and IEG Ratings Increased Dramatically in FY07

Source of rating	Share of projects rated moderately satisfactory or better		
	FY05	FY06	FY07
Bank's final Implementation Status and Results report (ISR)	87.9%	91.1%	93.0%
Bank's Implementation Completion and Results report (ICR)	85.7%	89.9%	83.3%
IEG's ICR review	80.8%	82.6%	75.8%
Difference between ISR and ICR review ratings—"disconnect"	*−7.1%*	*−8.5%*	*−17.2%*

Source: World Bank database.

Five factors have influenced weak project outcomes. forming loans, a finding also made by the World Bank's QAG (World Bank 2008a). For instance, two projects failed to recognize the importance of an appropriate legal and regulatory framework as a precondition to a privatization process. Several health projects failed to ensure a heightened focus on those interventions that would yield the greatest impact, leading, for instance, to inadequate targeting of the poor, the absence of a cost effective package of health services, or inadequate funding for behavior change interventions to prevent HIV/AIDS transmission among high-risk groups.

Second, overambition was a weakness. While project objectives were almost always relevant, a majority were too far-reaching. Sometimes this was in terms of assessing political commitment and the feasibility of certain reforms. Other times it was in assessing government effectiveness and capacity, or in requiring coordination across several ministries or cumbersome financial management procedures that were not manageable by the parties involved. IEG's evaluation of public sector reform (2008c) shows several examples where these factors led to unsatisfactory outcomes.

Third, delays in implementation caused difficulties, because circumstances changed and project design or implementation could not respond. About one-fifth of underperforming projects suffered from this problem.

Fourth, a majority of the unsatisfactory projects had a weak results framework with poor or no baseline data, making it difficult to assess the outcomes of the project, and outcomes were often not well linked to inputs and outputs.

Finally, various gaps in the Bank's own performance contributed to a lack of success. For example, despite being flagged by the QAG for poor quality at the outset, three projects were not reassessed or redesigned. The quality of the Bank's supervision was rated as moderately unsatisfactory or worse in two-thirds of all underperforming projects (and many such projects were not identified as problems in ongoing status reports). And Bank overall performance—as distinct from borrower performance or the effects of uncontrollable events—was ranked moderately unsatisfactory or worse in two-thirds of these problem projects, compared with only about one-fifth of the full sample. All of this points to a challenge in re-emphasizing a proactive quality control in management's attention to ongoing project performance.

How It Adds Up: Outcomes of Bank Country Programs

While Bank-supported projects have largely yielded positive development outcomes, country program outcomes—measured against their own objectives, which typically include growth, poverty reduction, and the environment—are far less satisfactory. Some previous assessments suggest that synergies between and among the Bank's lending, knowledge services, and dialogue are not fully exploited or that the projects are not always directly relevant to the country's core development challenges (World Bank 2008a; IEG 2006c).

The lower country-program ratings could also be influenced by other factors. The number and scale of the factors that affect broader country-level objectives is typically much greater than at the smaller-scale project level. Hence, outcomes measured at this level are more likely to be affected by pressures outside the control of development partners. It is also possible that objectives may be relatively more ambitious at the program rather than project level (and therefore less frequently attained) or indeed that it is more difficult to establish the connection between Bank inputs and outcomes at the program level (as opposed to at the project level).

Over the past 10 years, evaluations of 81 Bank country programs—incorporating projects, policy and technical advice, and other types of assistance—show that three-fifths of them were moderately satisfactory or better in meeting their development objectives. Looking at specific

Figure 2.4: CAEs Show Three-Fifths with Outcomes Moderately Satisfactory or Better

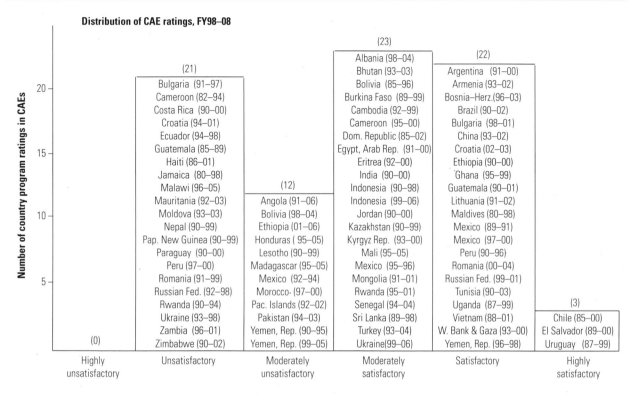

Distribution of CAE ratings, FY98–08

Number of country program ratings in CAEs

(21)
Bulgaria (91–97)
Cameroon (82–94)
Costa Rica (90–00)
Croatia (94–01)
Ecuador (94–98)
Guatemala (85–89)
Haiti (86–01)
Jamaica (80–98)
Malawi (96–05)
Mauritania (92–03)
Moldova (93–03)
Nepal (90–99)
Pap. New Guinea (90–99)
Paraguay (90–00)
Peru (97–00)
Romania (91–99)
Russian Fed. (92–98)
Rwanda (90–94)
Ukraine (93–98)
Zambia (96–01)
Zimbabwe (90–02)

(12)
Angola (91–06)
Bolivia (98–04)
Ethiopia (01–06)
Honduras (95–05)
Lesotho (90–99)
Madagascar (95–05)
Mexico (92–94)
Morocco· (97–00)
Pac. Islands (92–02)
Pakistan (94–03)
Yemen, Rep. (90–95)
Yemen, Rep. (99–05)

(23)
Albania (98–04)
Bhutan (93–03)
Bolivia (85–96)
Burkina Faso (89–99)
Cambodia (92–99)
Cameroon (95–00)
Dom. Republic (85–02)
Egypt, Arab Rep. (91–00)
Eritrea (92–00)
India (90–00)
Indonesia (90–98)
Indonesia (99–06)
Jordan (90–00)
Kazakhstan (90–99)
Kyrgyz Rep. (93–00)
Mali (95–05)
Mexico (95–96)
Mongolia (91–01)
Rwanda (95–01)
Senegal (94–04)
Sri Lanka (89–98)
Turkey (93–04)
Ukraine(99–06)

(22)
Argentina (91–00)
Armenia (93–02)
Bosnia–Herz.(96–03)
Brazil (90–02)
Bulgaria (98–01)
China (93–02)
Croatia (02–03)
Ethiopia (90–00)
Ghana (95–99)
Guatemala (90–01)
Lithuania (91–02)
Maldives (80–98)
Mexico (89–91)
Mexico (97–00)
Peru (90–96)
Romania (00–04)
Russian Fed. (99–01)
Tunisia (90–03)
Uganda (87–99)
Vietnam (88–01)
W. Bank & Gaza (93–00)
Yemen, Rep. (96–98)

(3)
Chile (85–00)
El Salvador (89–00)
Uruguay (87–99)

(0)

| Highly unsatisfactory | Unsatisfactory | Moderately unsatisfactory | Moderately satisfactory | Satisfactory | Highly satisfactory |

Outcome rating of county programs in CAEs

Source: IEG Country Assistance Evaluations.

Note: CAEs assess country program performance over a long period. Years in parentheses indicate the period that Bank country programs are assessed.

grades on IEG's ratings scale, as shown in figure 2.4 and table 2.3, the Bank succeeded in supporting satisfactory outcomes in 30 percent of evaluated programs; a further 30 percent of country programs were rated moderately satisfactory. But the remaining 40 percent of programs—concentrated in countries that are smaller or have extensive poverty, such as

Table 2.3: Summary of CAE Ratings, FY98–08

	MICs	LICs	All countries
Highly satisfactory	6%	0%	4%
Satisfactory	33%	18%	27%
Moderately satisfactory	25%	33%	28%
Moderately unsatisfactory	13%	18%	15%
Unsatisfactory	23%	30%	26%
Highly unsatisfactory	0%	0%	0%
Satisfactory and highly satisfactory	*39%*	*18%*	*31%*
Moderately satisfactory or better	*64%*	*51%*	*59%*

Source: IEG Country Assistance Evaluations.

Box 2.2: What Does a Satisfactory Country Program Look Like?

No single template exists for a satisfactory Bank-supported country program, since such programs vary greatly depending on the country's institutional capacity, stage of development, and particular development needs. The characteristics of the Indonesia country program illustrate some features of good outcomes found in several cases.

During fiscal 1999–2006, the Indonesia country program was largely successful. Bank support provided help to national authorities in securing economic recovery from the late 1990s economic crisis. By 2004, per capita income achieved precrisis levels, inflation fell to under 7 percent, and public debt was cut from nearly 100 percent of gross domestic product in 1999, to under 50 percent by 2005. These gains largely managed to turn around the effects of the crisis—the percentage of Indonesians living on less than one dollar per day was 16 percent in 2005, compared with 23 percent in 1999. The fall in income poverty and improvement in human development indicators were assisted by the Bank's work in community-driven development through the Kecamatan Development Program and by reconstruction following the 2004 tsunami. These achievements outweighed some areas in which outcomes from the Bank's program were less satisfactory—including in decentralization and fighting against corruption.

Outcomes of country programs are less satisfactory than project outcomes.

Malawi—were moderately unsatisfactory or worse in meeting their stated development objectives.

Very few country programs are producing best-practice results—indeed, of 36 programs rated since fiscal 2002, not one has been highly satisfactory. And among the 14 low-income countries (LICs) rated since fiscal 2002, not a single program has been rated satisfactory or better. At the same time, no program has ever been rated highly unsatisfactory.

Many programs in the largest countries that house the majority of the world's poor—including Brazil, China, India, Indonesia, and Mexico—were rated moderately satisfactory or better in their development outcomes. Box 2.2 shows such outcomes from the Indonesia country program. When country programs are weighted by the number of people in poverty (living on less than $2 per day), 86 percent of country programs are given a satisfactory rating. Even when excluding China and India, both above the line, the poverty-weighted satisfactory share is nearly two-thirds.

Few country programs have produced best-practice results.

There are also significant differences among subgroups of countries, as shown in table 2.3. Bank programs in MICs far outperform those in LICs. While IEG rated 39 percent of programs in MICs satisfactory or better, this was true of only 18 percent in LICs. Using a lower threshold, the difference is smaller but still substantial: 64 percent of ratings in MIC programs were moderately satisfactory or better, compared with 51 percent of ratings for LIC programs.

A less in-depth but more up-to-date snapshot of country program outcomes is provided by IEG reviews of Country Assistance Strategy Completion Reports (CASCRs). CASCR reviews differ from Country Assistance Evaluations (CAEs) in that they are a review of the Bank's own self-evaluation of its country assistance program and cover a shorter time period, typically three to five years, as compared with a decade or more in CAEs. CASCR review data, available since fiscal 2004, present a slightly more favorable assessment. Two-thirds of all programs reviewed were rated moderately satisfactory or better, as shown in figure 2.5 and table 2.4.[10] Here too, none of the country programs were rated highly unsatisfactory.

Consistent with the CAEs, higher ratings are almost entirely due to better outcomes in MICs than in LICs. More than three-fourths of the MICs had moderately satisfactory or better country outcomes, compared with half of LICs reviewed. And in only one MIC was Bank assistance rated unsatisfactory, as compared with four LICs, even though there were many more MICs in the sample.

Figure 2.5: CASCR Reviews Indicate That Bank Programs in MICs Outperform Those in LICs

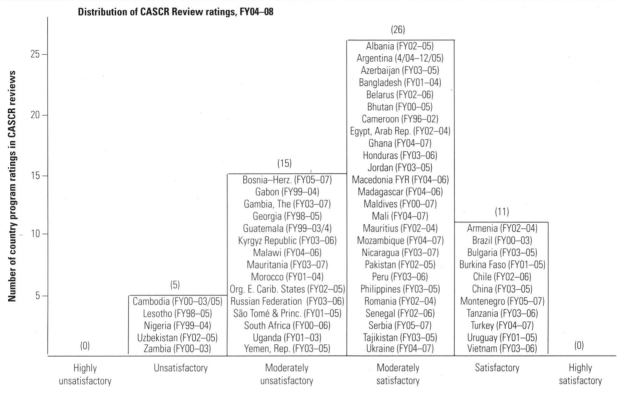

Distribution of CASCR Review ratings, FY04–08

Source: IEG reviews of Country Assistance Strategy Completion reports.
Note: CASCR Reviews cover a shorter period than CAEs. Years in parentheses indicate the period that Bank country programs are assessed.

Table 2.4: Summary of CASCR Review Ratings, FY03–08

	MICs	LICs	All countries
Highly satisfactory	0%	0%	0%
Satisfactory	22%	13%	18%
Moderately satisfactory	54%	39%	48%
Moderately unsatisfactory	22%	30%	26%
Unsatisfactory	3%	17%	8%
Highly unsatisfactory	0%	0%	0%
Satisfactory and highly satisfactory	*22%*	*13%*	*18%*
Moderately satisfactory or better	*76%*	*52%*	*66%*

Source: IEG reviews of Country Assistance Strategy Completion Reports.

Chapter 3

Evaluation Highlights

- The Bank's overall approach to M&E has many strengths.
- Progress has been made in updating policies and frameworks, but there is considerable room to improve how M&E is put into practice.
- At the project level, the overall quality of M&E is low.
- At the country level, results frameworks are increasingly produced but are often poorly formulated.
- The independence of external evaluations of global programs is improving, but their M&E systems are often weak.
- Impact evaluations are a useful addition, but topics need to be chosen strategically.

Child studying in public school in the Amazon region of Brazil; photo by Julio Pantoja, courtesy of the World Bank Photo Library.

Underpinning Impact—
M&E and Results Management

Monitoring and Evaluation Systems at the Project Level

The Bank's overall approach to M&E has many strengths (see appendix B for an overview). Indeed, its policies for monitoring and evaluating projects have been revised, to place greater emphasis on project outcomes. Specifically, the Bank:

- Required (a) investment projects to include results frameworks, outlining (final) project and intermediate outcomes as well as the process for carrying out M&E;[1] and (b) development policy operations to specify expected outcomes and measurable indicators for M&E in 2004 (World Bank 2004a).
- Replaced the Project Supervision Report with the Implementation Status and Results report (ISR) in 2005. The ISR now gives more prominence to project outcome and intermediate outcome indicators by including them in the main report, whereas in the past they were in an optional annex (infrequently updated).
- Harmonized the Bank and IEG's evaluation criteria for Implementation Completion and Results reports (ICRs) and IEG's ICR reviews in 2006. The procedures for programmatic development policy loan ICRs were also simplified to improve the effectiveness of the ICRs.

As part of the revisions, ICRs are now required to include an assessment of project M&E quality along three dimensions—design, implementation, and utilization. The review of M&E *design* examines the extent to which adequate indicators

were identified to monitor progress toward project development objectives. The assessment of M&E *implementation* is the extent to which appropriate data were actually collected, and *utilization* reviews the extent to which appropriate data were evaluated and used to inform decision making and resource allocation. IEG, as part of its ICR reviews, has started rating overall M&E quality using a four-point scale: high, substantial, modest, and negligible.[2] This quantitative assessment does not reflect a methodology that has been agreed to by Bank management; ICRs assess, but are not required to rate, M&E quality.

A review of the quality of project M&E showed a positive association between good project M&E and better project outcomes. It found that projects with highly satisfactory project outcome ratings had, on average, higher M&E quality rating (3.0 or equivalent to a rating of "substantial") compared with projects with unsatisfactory outcome ratings that had lower M&E quality (1.7 or equivalent to a rating of "negligible") as shown in (figure 3.1).

There is a positive association between good project M&E and better project outcomes, but the overall quality of project M&E is low.

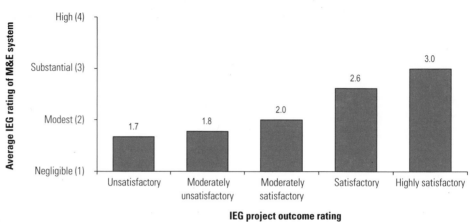

Figure 3.1: Projects with Higher Outcome Ratings Have Better M&E Ratings

Source: IEG.

But the overall quality of project M&E has been low. Of the 242 ICR reviews for which M&E quality ratings are available,[3] IEG rated that quality as modest or negligible in two-thirds of cases, as shown in figure 3.2. Poor design was a key factor in low M&E quality ratings. Some projects had weak results frameworks where the project outcomes were poorly defined and/or the link among the project outcomes, that is, the project development objectives, intermediate outcomes, and the project outputs was not clear. Another factor was poorly designed M&E

systems, where the monitoring indicators lacked baselines and targets and not enough attention was given to implementation.

Projects with high M&E quality ratings included M&E systems that were well designed, implemented, and used. The Second Rural Roads Project in Peru included performance monitoring indicators for outputs, intermediate outcomes, and outcomes that were conceptually clear, realistic, and measurable and were linked closely to the project's four main objectives. Impact evaluations were designed into the project, and the evaluation of the previous project provided the baseline for this project. The M&E framework also constituted an active learning process for the project's executing agency. The project was rated satisfactory for outcome. The Partnership for Polio Eradication Project in Pakistan was rated highly satisfactory for project outcome and high for M&E quality. The project was able to use existing systems, combined with substantial external technical and financial support, to develop a system and create demand for data, which are essential for disease eradication.

The impact of the changes in Bank M&E procedures may not yet be fully reflected in this analysis because most projects approved by the Board since fiscal 2005 are still under implemen-

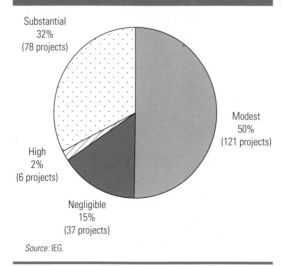

Figure 3.2: M&E Is Rated Modest or Lower in Two-Thirds of ICR Reviews

Substantial
32%
(78 projects)

Modest
50%
(121 projects)

High
2%
(6 projects)

Negligible
15%
(37 projects)

Source: IEG.

tation. Of the 242 projects with M&E quality ratings, 23 have been approved since fiscal 2005, of which 21 are development policy operations. Close to half (48 percent) of these projects were rated substantial or high for M&E quality. However, it is not clear whether this is due to better M&E quality ratings for development policy operations or because of improvements in M&E policies. A clearer picture will emerge in subsequent years as more projects from fiscal 2005 and afterward exit the portfolio and have ICRs and ICR reviews prepared.

It may not necessarily be policies and procedures, but rather a lack of incentives and priority that is constraining the design and use of M&E systems. As far back as 2000, a Bank working group on improving M&E found that M&E tended to be perceived as the least important of the dimensions of operational quality (World Bank 2000). Focus group participants for IEG consultations stated that they sometimes set ambitious development objectives and then faced difficulty linking them to projects, that there was excessive emphasis on quantitative data, and that monitor-

ing got less priority during implementation. Difficulties in M&E have also been highlighted in several IEG sector and thematic evaluations, as noted in box 3.1.

Many of these IEG findings are echoed in reports from the Bank's Quality Assurance Group. The QAG's most recent *Quality of Supervision (QSA7)* assessment noted satisfactory focus on management of inputs and outputs, but less so on outcomes (World Bank 2007a). The QAG's latest quality at entry assessment (World Bank 2008b) found improvements in results framework design (where more than 95 percent of the project were rated marginally satisfactory or better), but also observed that project development objective clarity and realism, consistency of project design with outcomes, and impact and outcome measurement could be improved. The Bank is proposing to strengthen monitoring under IDA15 by tracking the quality of the project development objectives at design and the adequacy of baselines during implementation (World Bank 2007b).

Poor M&E impairs the ability to manage ongoing projects and subsequently to evaluate them robustly.

Box 3.1: M&E Findings and Recommendations in Recent IEG Evaluations

IEG's evaluation of the World Bank's project-based and World Bank Institute training (IEG 2008d) found that Bank projects and the World Bank Institute both report on outputs (the number of people trained, the number of training days, participant satisfaction with training), but seldom on outcomes (changes in workplace behavior, institutional capacity development). It recommended that the Bank: (a) develop guidance and quality criteria for the design and implementation of training, to enable quality assurance and monitoring and evaluation of all its training support; and (b) improve the quality and impact of training by making available technical expertise on the design, implementation, and monitoring and evaluation of training to its staff and borrowers.

IEG's evaluation of World Bank assistance to agriculture in Sub-Saharan Africa (IEG 2007d) found that data systems and support for M&E have been insufficient to adequately inform the Bank's efforts to develop agriculture in Africa. M&E at the project level is often of limited value for answering fundamental outcome, impact, and efficiency questions, such as who benefited, which

crops received support and how, what has been the comparative cost effectiveness, and to what can one attribute gains. It recommended that the Bank improve data systems to better track activities it supports and strengthen M&E to report on project activities in various agro-ecological zones for different crops and farmer categories, including women.

IEG's recent evaluation of the Bank's Group's work in supporting environmental sustainability (IEG 2008a) recommended that the Bank Group, as a whole, improve its ability to monitor and evaluate the impact of its environment-related interventions. This included using current International Finance Corporation and Multilateral Investment Guarantee Agency evaluation systems as a starting point for betting monitoring for the whole Bank Group. It could further mobilize efforts for: (a) better baseline environmental assessment studies; (b) more holistic evaluation methods; (c) further development of environmental performance indicators; and (d) improved monitoring and reporting on project implementation and results.

Country-Level M&E: Early Evidence from Results-Based CASs

The Bank adopted the results-based Country Assistance Strategy (CAS) approach in 2005,[4] following a review that found that the evaluation framework remained the weakest area of the CAS, with the key issue being the "missing middle" between the CAS objectives and Bank operations (World Bank 2003a). A results-based CAS would be "a country assistance strategy that contains a strong orientation toward achieving realistic outcomes and results-oriented monitoring and evaluation system" (World Bank 2005a).

The Bank strengthened the results focus of its CASs.

The two main innovations of the results-based CAS approach were the CASCR as a self-evaluation tool and the results framework as a monitoring, management, and evaluation tool for the Bank country program. The results framework is expected to link higher-level country outcomes with Bank CAS outcomes, intermediate outcomes/milestones, and operations, and would include measurable indicators of progress that can be tracked through CAS implementation, encouraging active management and allowing both self- and independent evaluation (World Bank 2005a).

Experience with this new approach suggests that, so far, the CAS results framework typically has been used as a reference for evaluation, but not for monitoring or program management. This emerged from a review of results-based or results-oriented CASs and interviews with the Task Team Leaders of the reports to examine the extent the results framework was used for monitoring, management, and evaluation and to enhance the Bank's development effectiveness. CAS results frameworks served as an inventory of commitments in the CAS Progress Reports and were used to report on the status of CAS outcomes and/or intermediate outcomes without further analysis. The results framework was also used as a reference in evaluating the country program in the CASCRs, which included an annex with the current status of the CAS outcomes. One exception is Armenia, which in-

CAS results frameworks are used as a basis for evaluation but less so for country program monitoring and management.

corporated the CAS outcomes into their country portfolio performance review and is jointly managing the Bank program with the borrower to focus on CAS outcomes (box 3.2).

Poorly designed results frameworks limited their usefulness for country program monitoring and management. It is difficult to interpret the information on a project's status if the expected outcome is vaguely defined ("banking system financial capacity strengthened") and/or lacks baselines and targets to measure progress. Another issue is the volume of information to be provided. Assembling the data has proven challenging: the Task Team Leaders for the Progress and Completion Reports mentioned that they had to devote a significant amount of time and effort to collecting the data and updating the results framework. In some cases, the amount of information provided was overwhelming and yet failed to answer the basic question: "Is the Bank making sufficient progress toward achieving its CAS objectives." The Ghana Progress and Completion Reports addressed this issue by reporting actuals only for the 35 CAS monitoring indicators, which (except for those under the Governance Pillar) had baselines and targets.

IEG has also raised concerns over the poor design of CAS results frameworks. Many CAS

> **Box 3.2: Armenia Joint Country Portfolio Performance Review**
>
> As preparation for the 2007 CAS Progress Report, the Bank conducted a joint portfolio review with the government of Armenia, which covered not only the overall status of the portfolio, implementation issues, follow-up on previous commitments, and individual problem projects, but also the progress toward CAS objectives and the contribution of Bank instruments. Information was prepared on the status of 29 CAS outcomes and discussed with the government. Recommendations included specific steps, typically broader and policy-oriented, which are needed to improve project performance and to ensure achievement of CAS outcomes.

results frameworks had poorly articulated results chains—including in several IDA countries where the distinction between CAS outcomes and intermediate outcomes/milestones was unclear and the links between Bank products and CAS outcomes were poor. Many results frameworks had too many outcome measures—more than 40 CAS outcomes indicators and over 60 intermediate indicators—and/or lacked indicators with baselines and targets, making them less effective as a management and evaluation tool.

The lack of outcome data makes it more difficult to assess the achievement of Bank CAS objectives in the CASCR reviews. While most of the CASs reviewed to date were prepared before the results-based CASs were introduced, some did include expected outcomes and/or results frameworks that were retrofitted in the CASCRs. IEG reviewers noted that the CASCRs discussed what the Bank did (process, inputs and outputs), but did not necessarily provide convincing evidence of the success of the Bank country program in achieving its objectives.

Whether staff have the right incentives to promote effective results-based frameworks for CASs remains open to question. In interviews for this report, some Task Team Leaders talked of the difficulty of getting support from their sector colleagues when updating the information in the CAS results frameworks. Some sector staff did not see value in the monitoring indicators because they were not involved in the formulation of the original CAS results framework. Given the demands on their time, monitoring of the CAS results framework and analyzing Bank country performance gets low priority, reflecting some skepticism about the value added by the exercise. This echoes findings from previous IEG evaluations (IEG 2004a, 2006d) which concluded that "getting results" was not yet part of the reward system for individual staff and that the Bank's incentives rewarded the work that the staff do at the early stages of the project cycle—that is, preparing new operations—more highly than work at the later stages of supervision, such as evaluation and learning lessons.

One of the lessons learned from the Progress Report and CASCRs was the need to better align Bank activities with CAS outcomes. The Armenia CAS Progress Report noted that it is better to build the results framework around Poverty Reduction Strategy Paper outcomes and indicators. Baselines are important and other indicators should be sought if baseline data are not available, and data sources should be verified to make sure that information can be made available in a timely manner. The Ghana CASCR observed that one of the weaknesses was that some indicators were only indirectly related to Bank interventions. The Mozambique CASCR also commented on the importance of the Poverty Reduction Strategy Paper, but noted that the CAS should set more realistic targets, distinguishing them from Poverty Reduction Strategy Paper targets and choosing such targets only if they are related to the Poverty Reduction Support Credit (PRSC) or where the Bank is the main source of support to achieve the Poverty Reduction Strategy Paper target.

Another lesson was the importance of strengthening M&E capacity at the sector or project level. The Mozambique CASCR noted that projects also need to strengthen their monitoring of results, and focus on helping sectors to develop monitoring and evaluation systems, which would help project data collection and reporting. The Bosnia-Herzegovina CASCR made a similar point, noting that the focus on results should go beyond Bank-financed operations and that the Bank teams should help their counterparts to develop appropriate results frameworks for all their operations.

Linking the CAS and project results frameworks and strengthening the country's capacity to conduct M&E would not only reduce the cost of data collection, but also increase its relevance and use.

While the discussion focused on countries with CASs, M&E is also important in Low-Income

Poor design limited the usefulness of the results frameworks for Bank's country programs.

Incentives favoring project preparation and delivery over M&E continue to be a concern.

It is important to link CAS and project results frameworks, and strengthen country capacity to conduct M&E.

M&E is just as critical in Low-Income Countries Under Stress. Countries Under Stress (LICUS), which are covered by Interim Strategy Notes or Transitional Support Strategies. An IEG evaluation (2006e) concluded that M&E is just as critical, maybe more so, in LICUS (box 3.3).

Going forward, country teams should examine results chains and explore synergies among various interventions in country programs (projects, analytic and advisory activities, trust-funded activities, and so on) to identify shared higher-level outcomes. This could lead to a reduction in the number of country outcomes to be measured, making the frameworks more strategically focused and usable. Teams could also identify areas where the project results framework could be linked into the CAS results framework. Establishing synergies between interventions and identifying possible gaps in the Bank program could go toward reducing the disconnect between country and project portfolio outcomes.

The Bank could take steps to strengthen the results frameworks and better manage for results.

The basics need to be ensured. CAS results frameworks need to have monitoring indicators with baselines and targets to measure progress.

Systems need to be in place to ensure that the information is collected. This may require trading off data availability with desirability.

Finally, integrating the CAS results framework into Bank operational procedures would establish the use of the performance data and could provide an incentive to update and utilize the CAS results framework. There are some pilots under way. At the country level, the Moldova Country Management Unit is piloting a scorecard to link CAS outcomes, operational performance, and Bank budget allocation (box 3.4). At the regional level, the East Asia and Pacific Region piloted and is expanding an approach to link the achievement of CAS objectives with budget allocation (box 3.4). Linking Bank resource allocation with progress toward CAS outcomes would also provide an incentive to monitor and analyze Bank country performance indicators. The Bank could learn from and build on these pilots.

Managing Global Programs and Partnerships: An Emerging Agenda

The Bank has put in place new business processes for global programs and partnerships (GPPs), which recognize these as a separate product line of the Bank, and which aim to integrate GPP business processes and information with the Bank's regular operational business systems (IEG 2004b). Throughout their life cycle, GPPs now follow procedures similar to a simplified lending process—using familiar concepts and systems and allowing new GPPs to be tracked from their start through to evaluation and results assessment.

Enhanced processes have also been put in place to encourage greater selectivity although their effect remains to be assessed fully. Proposals for new GPPs and requests for new Development Grant Facility (DGF) funding are now presented in a standard Partnership Review Note and considered, based on input from relevant parties in a review meeting chaired by a director. The GPP Group and the Legal Department are providing early advice to task teams with regard to governance, which focuses on the quality of the governance structure (how the partners will form the partnership and interact with each other),

---

Box 3.3: Results Measurement and Monitoring in LICUS

Monitoring and evaluation are at least as important in LICUS as they are in any other country. Monitoring and evaluation are crucial in LICUS for a number of reasons. First, the Bank, like other donors, is still learning what approaches work in LICUS contexts. Closely monitoring experiences in order to draw lessons is critical, and learning and sharing needs to become a more prominent feature of LICUS work. Second, given that progress is often slow in these countries, it is important to reassess continually whether the program is on course to achieve the desired outcomes. Third, a constantly changing and volatile LICUS environment where progress is often nonlinear means that program adaptation is essential—closely tracking performance will help determine when and what kind of adaptation is necessary. Effective learning-by-doing to improve the Bank's future effectiveness in LICUS can only happen with strong monitoring and evaluation.

Source: IEG 2006e.

Box 3.4: Use of CAS Results Frameworks in Country Program Management

Moldova Results Scorecard

The Moldova Country Management Unit is developing a Moldova Results Scorecard which will integrate, in one place, the different elements of country program management: progress toward country strategic outcomes, lending and delivery costs of analytic and advisory activities, and quality (QAG and IEG assessments). The scorecard will be used to link country program management and resource allocation and improve program and project results.

Strategically Managing Country Programs in East Asia

The East Asia and Pacific Region piloted the use of CAS results frameworks to increase management accountability for results. The new approach is grounded in CASs and, at the same time, focused across core Regional priorities and actionable milestones. It is intended to be consistent across Regional and country levels and enables Regional aggregation to allow discussion with senior management. Country teams took their respective CAS results frameworks, agreed on the critical CAS outcomes where they would focus their efforts, and narrowed the monitoring indicators to a manageable number in a one-page table. This information was used in the annual and midyear program/strategy discussions.

---

legitimacy, the voice of developing countries, and the Bank's roles (particularly whether the Bank's accountability and responsibility are aligned with the Bank's formal authority and actual control). A new results framework and performance indicators were added to the Partnership Review Note and the DGF Progress Report on a voluntary basis in fiscal 2007, and made compulsory in fiscal 2008.

Quality-at-entry reviews of DGF-supported programs by QAG also provide feedback that contributes to enhanced selectivity. QAG noted several improvements in fiscal 2007, as compared with fiscal 2006, including stronger quality of program design and improved readiness for implementation, as well as a number of areas needing improvement, such as unrealistic objectives, weak results frameworks, and poor documentation.

Taken together, these represent a substantial improvement over the previous partnership approval and tracking system for GPPs, which was not integrated into the Bank's regular operational business systems. However, to date the improvements have mainly occurred with respect to DGF-supported programs, since these programs have to comply with the new business processes in order to receive grants. Except for DGF grants received, the financial information in the Bank's databases (on the sources and uses of funds for each program) is not complete or reliable. None of

the Bank's existing information systems include financial resources that are not channeled through the Bank, and the Bank's Task Team Leaders are not required to provide or update this information on an annual basis.

The requirement for all programs receiving DGF funding of $300,000 or more, over the life of the program, to undertake an independent evaluation every three to five years has led to an increasing number of program-level evaluations. However, the Bank has not yet extended this requirement to the many other programs not receiving DGF support, as previously recommended by IEG (2002), though it is currently revising the relevant Operational Policy to achieve this. Implementing such a requirement should be fairly straightforward for programs supported by Bank-administered trust funds. For programs that are not supported either by the DGF or by Bank-administered trust funds, the Bank should still use its influence, as a member of the governing body, to encourage periodic independent evaluations.

The independence of external evaluations is improving. Out of the first seven evaluations that IEG reviewed, five were executed independent of the management of the program, and without

Bank management has put in place new business processes that aim to integrate GPPs with the Bank's regular business.

Feedback from QAG quality-at-entry reviews of DGF-supported programs is contributing to enhanced selectivity.

The independence of external evaluations is improving. apparent conflicts of interest. The governing bodies generally commissioned the evaluation, approved the terms of reference, managed the selection process, and reviewed the draft report independent of program management. In four out of these five cases, the selection of the external evaluators was competitive.

However, the quality of three of the seven was compromised by a weak M&E system for the program. Either the objectives and strategies of the program were not well defined (too diffuse, process-oriented, difficult to measure, or open to different interpretations by different stakeholders), the M&E system was not well designed (focusing only on inputs and outputs, and not outcomes), or the data on the progress of activities and on the achievement of outcomes were not systematically collected. And in three of the seven programs an inadequate budget did not permit any fieldwork to verify facts on the ground or elicit the perceptions of implementers and beneficiaries in developing countries. As a result, neither the external evaluations nor IEG found much systematic evidence relating to the achievement of the seven programs' objectives at the outcome level, and it is difficult to say whether the $100 million spent on the programs annually ultimately had a substantial effect on the ground.

The quality of some evaluations was compromised by a weak M&E system for the program.

External evaluations are influencing the strategic directions and designs of GPPs. Notwithstanding these shortcomings, the external evaluations have had significant impacts on the programs reviewed. The evaluation led to a revision in the strategic direction or design of the program in six out of seven cases. The evaluation led to a change in the governance of the program in four cases, and led directly to continued or increased funding in four cases.

Improving Our Understanding of Causality: The Use of Impact Evaluations

In response to the pressures for accountability, the development community in recent years has accorded increasing attention to impact evaluation as another tool for generating knowledge about the effectiveness of development interventions. The challenge now is how best to use this approach for increasing knowledge regarding development issues, advancing the broader results agenda, and stimulating client engagement in, and capacity for, monitoring and evaluation.

The results agenda can potentially benefit from impact evaluations, although they are clearly not a panacea. Impact evaluations explicitly identify a counterfactual through experimental or quasi-experimental designs to measure the true impact of development interventions. Accurate measurement of results can help for efficient allocation of resources and effective project/policy selection and design. The potential benefits of an impact evaluation extend beyond any particular project or program because the evaluation can provide information and lessons for the broader development community. It is possible, therefore, that impact evaluations may be underfunded unless there is explicit support from management and clients. On the other hand, it must be recognized that impact evaluations are highly specific to the context and often quite costly to launch, and their benefits are uncertain until they are completed.

The number of impact evaluations at the Bank has grown rapidly recently, with a rise from 60 under way in 2006, to 158 in mid-2008.[5] Yet, the evaluations are concentrated in a few sectors and topics. Almost 70 percent of the ongoing evaluations are clustered in five areas, as shown in figure 3.3, and three of these—education, health, and conditional cash transfers (many of which also focus on education outcomes)—also comprise the top categories of previously completed evaluations. There is also a concentration by Region, with nearly two-thirds of ongoing evaluations located in Sub-Saharan Africa and South Asia (see figure 3.4).

Why evaluations are concentrated in certain areas and whether the observed distribution is efficient are questions for Bank management. Some substantive areas are more amenable to impact evaluations, and Bank clients differ in their receptivity to evaluations. But staff incentives may

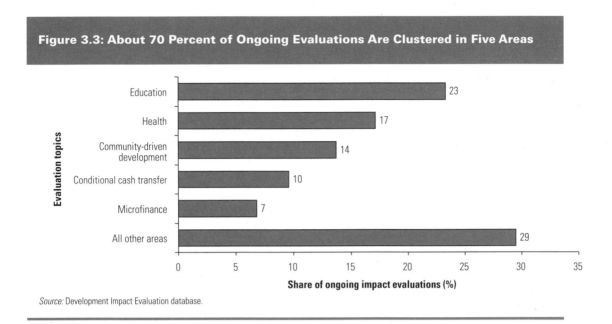

Figure 3.3: About 70 Percent of Ongoing Evaluations Are Clustered in Five Areas

Source: Development Impact Evaluation database.

also play an important role, and care must be taken not to overexamine some topics while others are underresearched. In an ideal setting, the decision to fund impact evaluations in a given area would take into account one or more of the following five criteria: the value of answering the question in terms of benefits and costs of a specific project, the value of answering the question for other current or future projects, the cost of the evaluation, the innovative nature of the project, and the likely feasibility of designing a convincing impact evaluation.

The Bank has the capacity and resources to be a global leader in using impact evaluations to drive effective development assistance. Required steps include identifying important gaps in our knowledge; closing these gaps with effective and replicated evaluations; leveraging knowledge from impact evaluations through effective discussion, dissemination, and application across the institution; and shifting expenditures from unsuccessful to successful interventions. Clients should be closely engaged and ideally, in many

Impact evaluations are not a panacea, but they are an important part of the results agenda.

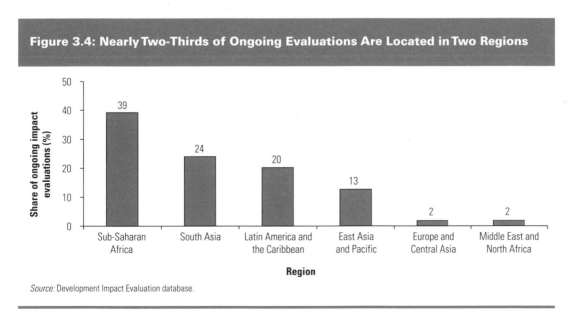

Figure 3.4: Nearly Two-Thirds of Ongoing Evaluations Are Located in Two Regions

Source: Development Impact Evaluation database.

Impact evaluation topics should be chosen strategically and the results should influence future funding decisions.

cases, leading the process of implementing evaluations and learning from their findings. A major challenge facing the Bank is to assess and compare the relative effectiveness of alternative interventions rather than largely assessing the effectiveness of different ways of implementing a given intervention. Existing initiatives, such as the Development Impact Evaluation Initiative, have made some progress toward these goals.

IEG itself is aiming to increase its own use of impact evaluations and capacity to review impact evaluations within the Bank. Through meta-evaluations and mixed methods approaches, impact evaluations provide important opportunities to enhance IEG's evaluation role.

Monitoring Institutional Effectiveness

The development community is focusing on results on the ground, with the Millennium Development Goals serving as a common framework. In 2002, the heads of the multilateral development banks issued a joint statement on their commitment to scale up their work on measuring, monitoring, and managing for results, following the Monterrey Conference on Financing for Development.

The development community is focused on results on the ground and is interested in the impact of Bank operations.

The IDA15 replenishment negotiations distilled this focus on results in a very real way. During the negotiations, the Bank faced competition for donor funding from different organizations and programs, many of them focused on specific issues. Donor governments had to answer to their citizens on the effective use of their resources and therefore requested that IDA demonstrate that it was achieving results on the ground and what those results were. IDA's competition often focuses on single issues—such as children, health, and the environment—and are better able to present aggregated output data (such as numbers of beneficiaries assisted, goods provided, and so on) and to describe their results. The Bank, on the other hand, carries out not only projects but also additional activities, such as policy

The IDA Results Monitoring System and AfricaRMS provide a broader view of results, but not for all countries.

and institutional development or donor coordination; impacts are harder to measure and attribute to the Bank. In response, the report "Additions to IDA Resources: Fifteenth Replenishment" (World Bank 2008c) served to illustrate accomplishments in individual projects, sectors, and countries, thus complementing the information provided in the IDA Results Measurement System (RMS).

The IDA RMS assesses Bank-wide performance, but only for IDA countries. The RMS has two tiers. *Tier 1* focuses on monitoring country outcomes and includes 14 country outcome indicators that are consistent with the Millennium Development Goals, are priorities in poverty reduction strategies, and reflect IDA's activities. These are high-level country outcomes that are influenced by the Bank, but for which the Bank is not solely responsible. *Tier 2* monitors IDA's effectiveness. It consists of indicators: (a) at the country level, where the cumulative introduction of results-based CASs in IDA countries is monitored; (b) at the project level, where four project quality indicators are monitored; and (c) outputs from completed projects in fours sectors (health, education, water supply, and rural transport).

IDA prepared a progress report on the RMS in 2007 and made suggestions for improved monitoring under IDA15. It reported, among other things, that IDA had built 7,500 km of road, trained 81,400 health professionals and 282,500 teachers, and made 87,000 new water connections based on IDA project ICRs in fiscal 2006–07. The report concluded that the introduction of the RMS "has generated a sharper focus on results at the country level and a stronger internal results culture." It also acknowledged that internal process weaknesses remain in the quality of Tier 2 outcome indicators and the availability of baselines for all outcome indicators at entry in IDA projects. IDA recognized that because "many ICRs still lack figures on outputs, or report them in a variety of forms (different units, no standard categories), aggregation remains very challenging." For IDA15, the report proposed that IDA track the quality of the project development objectives at design, the adequacy of baselines during implementation, and the reporting quality of outputs and outcomes in ICRs, based on the original results framework as part of Tier 2. The report also suggested including ratings on CAS implementation from IEG's CASCR reviews to measure the quality of Bank country programs.

The Africa Region developed the Africa Results Monitoring System (AfricaRMS) as a comprehensive online system in the Bank for monitoring on-the-ground results of Bank activities. It consists of a set of harmonized project and country indicators to facilitate counting and aggregating results at the country, sector, Region, and Bank-wide levels. AfricaRMS partnered with the education, malaria, HIV, water, private sector development, governance, agriculture, energy, and roads teams to build monitoring frameworks that are fully aligned with existing global initiatives. It also includes write-ups to tell the story behind the numbers, describing how good results are changing people's lives, and descriptions of impact evaluations carried out in Africa. The AfricaRMS is aligned with the Africa Action Program.

The goal of the AfricaRMS is to use select information to show the results of Bank operations and development progress for both the Region and individual countries. It not only helps teams focus on achieving results but also provides internal and external clients access to live information about stories from projects and beneficiaries, impact evaluation results, and data for priority sectors.

The system is still being refined and faces several challenges. The Region is working to improve the availability of country data and harmonized indicator measurement across Bank operations. It is also making efforts to better integrate financial data, and output and outcome data from operations at the sector and country level. Measurement systems across countries and among development partners will also need to be harmonized.

IEG's mandate is to evaluate the outcome of Bank-supported projects and programs, as measured against their objectives, and its work—including ARDE 2008—obviously represents a part of the Bank Group's efforts to monitor institutional effectiveness. An assessment of IEG's effectiveness, including the perspectives of its clients and the extent to which its recent recommendations have been implemented, can be found in appendix C.

Chapter 4

Man sifting seeds along the Red River in northern Vietnam; photo by Quy-Toan Do, courtesy of the World Bank Photo Library.

Lessons and Opportunities

Practical Lessons for the Near Term

Some practical lessons emerge from this analysis. The increasing disconnect between Bank and IEG project ratings needs to be reversed by renewing attention to project reporting and self-assessments consistent with standards set by IEG. The drop in 2007 project ratings also must be watched carefully.

To improve the focus on results, steps are needed: (a) at the project level and in global and regional programs, to enhance the quality of the M&E systems, especially by working to put in place good baseline information, to elucidate clearly the link between project outputs and targeted outcomes, and to extend evaluation requirements to global programs beyond those supported by DGF; (b) at the country level, to simplify results frameworks and thus make them more useful in guiding and evaluating programs; and (c) at the institutional level for the Bank and in partner countries, to manage and learn from a growing number of impact evaluations, including by better integrating them into country programs and exploiting cross-country synergies in conducting and sharing studies.

Directions for the Overall Bank Agenda

The development community's focus on results on the ground has also generated interest in the Bank's overall development impact. The IDA15 replenishment exercise reinforced the importance of articulating the results (both outputs and outcomes) of Bank operations to donors and other external stakeholders.

Despite increased international interest, the Bank is not yet well positioned to articulate the results of its interventions. The IDA RMS and the AfricaRMS aim to report on the Bank's achievements in a systematic manner, but for a specific set of countries. The Bank is considering a corporate-level results report, which is expected to synthesize the Bank's contribution to results, in place of the Sector Strategy Implementation Update.

The experience of developing M&E systems at the project and country level, and for the IDA RMS and AfricaRMS, provides lessons and challenges for developing a Bank-wide results report, including:

- Performance measures should be limited to a manageable number that capture the critical elements reflecting development effectiveness and can be measured and monitored rigorously.
- A monitoring system should be designed not only to report on results but also to manage for results, that is, to collect performance information to assess whether the Bank is on track to achieve its corporate strategic objectives, make changes where needed, and allocate resources. Opera-

tional use of the performance measures would provide an incentive for managers and staff to organize, collect, and analyze the data.

- The Bank would need to ensure that its information systems are aligned, to supply the information and minimize the data assembly costs, for example, by standardizing project and country performance indicators as much as possible (a move already under way in the Africa Region and in several networks).

PART II

Shared Global Challenges
Lessons from the Bank's Experience

Chapter 5

Evaluation Highlights

- Development issues that involve international collective action, such as climate protection, present some of the greatest challenges of our time.
- Fostering global public goods is now one of the Bank's six strategic priorities.
- The differing nature of the various GPGs influences the way in which the Bank and its development partners address them.

Satellite image of hurricane; photo ©Adastra/ Getty Images, reproduced by permission.

The Challenge of Global Public Goods

In an era of rapid globalization, the importance of coordinated global solutions to cross-border problems has risen in tandem. In recent years there has been enormous growth in international attention to climate change, avian flu, international trade agreements, and other supranational issues collectively known as global public goods.

Many important GPGs—whose key characteristics are highlighted in box 5.1—need collective action across countries to be delivered effectively. This applies, for example, to keeping the air clean or concerted campaigns against communicable diseases. Individual countries may not have the incentive or wherewithal to take action, and thus GPGs can be chronically undersupplied even when there is widespread recognition of the urgency of worldwide action.

The Bank, for its part, is taking steps to address some of these issues. In previous decades, while most of the Bank's financial and advisory support was about providing public goods, it was traditionally focused at the country level, on national public goods such as public health, regulatory frameworks, and the provision of infrastructure. More recently, the Bank has increasingly been called upon to help in the supply of public goods that transcend borders.

Box 5.1: Key Characteristics of Global Public Goods

Economists describe pure public goods as "nonrival" and "nonexcludable." Nonrival means the supply of the good, such as clean air, to one person (or country) does not lead to there being less of it for another. Nonexcludable means that once the good is provided for one person, it is available for all to benefit from it. Typically, at the margin, the net benefits accruing to private individuals from such goods are less than the net benefits for society as a whole, and hence the public good is undersupplied in private markets. Public goods require collective action to be properly provided and, at the national level, this can often be coordinated by using government powers (including taxation, spending, and regulation).

Importantly, public goods also have a spatial dimension. Their geographic reach runs across a continuum from local community boundaries, to national borders, to regions of several countries, to the global sphere. The usual problems in supplying public goods are exacerbated for truly global public goods. That is because there is a divergence between the costs and benefits captured at the national and global levels, and it is particularly difficult to secure collective action across countries.

To this end, the World Bank Group president has promoted the fostering of GPGs as one of the Bank's six strategic pillars (World Bank 2007c). And the Development Committee endorsed a new framework for the role of the Bank in this arena in October 2007 (World Bank 2007d). The World Bank Global Public Goods Working Group has been appointed to take forward the president's strategic pillar. Further steps are needed for the Bank to achieve its objectives outlined in the framework.

It is important to recognize that the variety of GPGs have very different features, as discussed in more detail in appendix D. From a demand side, when viewed from an individual country perspective, some have benefits that are closely aligned to national interest (for example, the control of HIV/AIDS). In others, such as protecting the earth's climate by reducing emissions of greenhouse gases, there is a great divergence between national and global benefits. Part of the Bank's role—particularly in advocacy work and in providing grant finance—can be viewed as a way of "internalizing the externality" and bringing national and global demand for GPGs closer together.

Global public goods have different features, which has implications for the way the Bank deals with them.

From a supply side, GPGs also have different characteristics. Some require only one or a few countries to be involved in their supply, whereas others need all countries to be active (for example, ensuring the participation of a country that would, otherwise, be the weakest link in a strategy to stop the spread of a communicable disease). Some GPGs require many donors to be involved—opportunities for the Bank to use its convening power—while the supply of others may rest with other major public and private institutions.

The differing nature of GPGs therefore has implications for the way in which the Bank (and other bodies) deals with them. The Bank, as a global institution with considerable reach, is potentially well positioned to help the international community work at all levels in fostering GPGs. The Bank claims (World Bank 2007d) its comparative advantage in fostering GPGs is that it can:

- Work with countries to help them integrate GPGs into their national policies and programs as well as country assistance strategies, analytical and advisory activities, and lending.
- Display constructive advocacy by using its research and analytical capacity to communicate the perspectives and interests of developing countries in international arenas.
- Be an active partner in responding to global challenges and a source of innovative financing mechanisms.

Putting such comparative advantage into action has posed challenges for the Bank and its partners. The Bank has focused on five identified GPG clusters: preserving the environmental commons, controlling communicable diseases, enhancing the participation of developing countries in the global trading system, strengthening the international financial architecture, and creating and sharing knowledge relevant for development (World Bank 2007d).

This report examines the ways in which the Bank's country-based model helps or hinders its support for GPGs. Given the breadth of the topic—spanning numerous programs and virtually all sectors—and the lack of comprehensive evaluative evidence, this report is necessarily a partial stocktaking of the situation. It pays special attention to evidence on experiences with two of the most prominent GPG themes—the environmental commons and communicable diseases—and refers to other examples (including trade) where the context and available information warrants. The closing chapters review the Bank's experience as an advocate for action on GPGs and draw overall lessons for the Bank as it develops its approach in this area.

Chapter 6

Evaluation Highlights

- Systems for integrating GPGs into country strategies are under-developed.
- Attention to GPGs gets diluted as it moves from the Bank's corporate strategy to lower levels.
- Bank administrative spending on GPGs is among the smallest for its six priorities, and the growing role of trust funds presents challenges.
- Concessional finance is important to foster many GPGs.
- A mismatch between country needs and global ambitions for GPGs limits the use of the country model, especially without an attractive financial instrument.

Wind turbine farm; photo ©Frank Whitney/ Getty Images, reproduced by permission.

Using the Bank's Country-Based Model to Foster Global Public Goods: Does It Work?

How It Works in Theory—the Bank's Strategic Setting for Fostering Global Public Goods

Relying on the country-based model as the platform for the Bank's work on GPGs is a double-edged sword. Why? Because the Bank's systems largely mirror international structure, giving primacy—for obvious reasons—to national decision making on policies and programs supported by the Bank. GPGs that permit significant benefits to be captured at the country level—and so global and national interests coincide—are best suited for the Bank's country-based model.

Country directors and their teams are able to work in the traditional way with their counterparts to develop approaches supported by the Bank, be it through knowledge, convening power, or finance.

When a GPG has benefits, however, which are not easily or meaningfully appropriated at the national level (for example, cleaner air provided as a result of more energy-efficient production technologies), or where the costs of providing the GPG fall disproportionately on an individual country (for example, income foregone by not using forest resources), then the country model comes under strain. Staff interviews confirm that country directors and their teams do not have the incentive to advance an agenda that does not

directly appeal to their counterparts. Nor do they typically have the internal budget or instruments to be able to do so effectively.[1] In short, it is difficult to bridge the gap between global needs and country preferences.

Experience with Bank Country Assistance Strategies

Country Assistance Strategies[2] for partner nations define proposed country programs and form the bedrock of the Bank's overall engagement with developing countries. Moreover, because a great deal of the Bank's work, particularly its financing and knowledge services, is explicitly incorporated into individual CASs, such strategies are of pivotal importance as a starting point for the Bank's work in connecting global

Systems for integrating GPGs into CASs are underdeveloped and worth upgrading.

and country issues. What does experience tell us about how GPGs are playing out in country strategies?

The templates for compiling a CAS do not make explicit reference to global programs or GPGs as issues that must be considered. Likewise, templates for CAS Completion Reports and IEG's own Country Assistance Evaluations do not give explicit guidance on GPG issues. This may well be a gap worthy of further review. The Bank's internal CAS review process does allow for draft material to be circulated for comment to various parts of the Bank beyond the specific country team, including relevant groups involved with GPGs, such as the Sustainable Development Network and the Bank's Global Programs and Partnerships (GPP) unit. This process gives some opportunity for that perspective on GPGs to be added. It is not common, however, for experts from the centrally based anchor units (in the Bank networks) to be active members of the CAS preparation team.

Which GPGs feature strongly in Bank country strategies? A review of major recent CASs found that the environmental commons is the GPG most frequently noted explicitly in country strategies. Climate change, air pollution, and carbon emissions are reported (in the vast majority of CASs) as being addressed through the Bank's own lending or analytic and advisory activities, the Global Environment Facility (GEF) or the carbon funds. This observation resonates with IEG's earlier evaluation of MICs (IEG 2007a), which found that mention and integration of global programs in CASs was more likely for those close to the Bank such as the GEF and the carbon funds.

Environmental commons is the GPG noted most frequently in country strategies.

Attention to communicable diseases is the second most frequently emphasized GPG in CASs. But in examining CASs it is often difficult to determine whether work on communicable diseases is primarily focused on national interests (and national goods) or whether the interests of the wider global community are also driving or influencing the Bank's stance. In about

70 percent of CASs reviewed, the documents mention work on either HIV/AIDS, tuberculosis, malaria, or avian flu—which might be taken as the upper bound of attention on these GPG issues. About one-third of the CASs reviewed mention Bank support for national disease surveillance systems.

This pattern has been confirmed in interviews with Bank country directors and their staff.[3] They report that they are open to considering and including important GPG issues in their dialogue with counterparts and, ultimately, in core country strategies. When the Bank is able to draw a practical connection between a GPG and the poverty focus of the Bank, it has a base upon which to build. The key then is to exploit the comparative advantage of combining the Bank's global and local knowledge, because it is the mix of the two that allows the greatest added value to be delivered to the client. But country directors report two significant drawbacks in delivering these potential benefits.

First, many respondents argue that, in a nutshell, "the networks are not working." From their perspective, the Bank's centralized anchor units have not been providing the valuable cross-country research, expertise, and support needed to help foster GPGs at the individual country level. In part, this may reflect gaps in the Bank's own global knowledge but respondents also suggested it was a problem of ineffective dissemination (internally, and to external audiences) of global expertise and research. This last theme is a recurring one—several evaluations from IEG and others have drawn attention to continuing flaws in the way the Bank transmits its analytical and research work (IEG 2007a).

Second, country directors remain concerned about what, at times, appears to be a bewildering array of global programs with which the Bank is associated. In some instances, the information made available on global programs is so voluminous and broad that it is difficult for country teams to digest and use. In other cases, some global programs (and their internal sponsors) circumvent the normal country dialogue approach, and foist their agenda onto the national dialogue. Many country directors appeal for a rationalized approach that tailors information from global programs much more carefully to country circumstances, which would facilitate a stronger engagement over the long term.

With the Bank's increased attention at the corporate level to GPGs, has there been a similar increase in coverage of GPGs in CASs? This report reviewed a relevant sample of countries in which the Bank has significant engagement and for which recent and historic CASs are available. In sum, there does not seem to be enough evidence to say that the treatment of any of the main GPGs is significantly different in the most recent CASs from their earlier equivalents. In fact, the picture is rather mixed. For example, the latest Vietnam CAS and Brazil Country Partnership Strategy (CPS) seem to address GPGs in a more extended fashion than earlier strategies. In Pakistan, the treatment is similar between the two CAS periods, as is also the case for the China CAS (which has had reasonably good coverage over an extended period).

One important issue highlighted by staff in country and network positions is the differing time horizons that apply in different strategies. Country strategies typically cover two to four years, which has to be aligned with national pressures (often including electoral cycles). Yet, global strategies to deal with GPGs have time horizons sometimes measured in decades, and implementation measures typically for five years or more. This "mismatch of time horizons" poses an overarching problem for bringing public policy to bear on medium- and long-term global challenges. It is also a source of tension reflected in the country-level client dialogue and priorities across different groups (for example, country teams and anchor specialists) within the Bank. How to make a more effective link between available short-term instruments and medium-term challenges deserves further consideration (IEG 2008a).

The latest Brazil CPS[4] provides a very good example of clear and prominent integration of GPG themes in country-level strategies (see box 6.1).

The Experience with Bank Network (Sector) and Regional Strategies

Given the sporadic attention to GPGs in country strategies, are strategies above the country level providing more attention to GPGs? That is the case with regard to corporate-level strategy, where the Bank has paid significant attention to GPGs, most notably in the GPG Framework (World Bank 2007d) and Long-Term Strategic Exercise (World Bank 2007e). But these strate-

There is no evidence that the treatment of GPGs in CASs has expanded across-the-board over time.

Box 6.1: Brazil: A Best Practice in Integrating GPG Themes in Country Strategies

The latest Brazil CPS is unique among the CASs reviewed in this ARDE for its treatment of GPG issues. The partnership strategy explicitly references GPGs and particularly highlights the inherent tension in promoting GPGs at the country level:

The Bank will engage with Brazil with climate change, trade, and other global public goods issues. In so doing, the Bank will help to ensure that Brazil's perspectives and interests are represented, in ensuring that the line between global goods and national ownership is not blurred, in ensuring that development needs are given equal billing. In short, the Bank's perspectives will be to 'level the playing field' on global public goods.

Brazil is special for its *central role in dealing with many global public goods (including AIDS, climate change, biodiversity, and clean energy and for the fact that it is a demanding borrower that 'pushes the Bank to the next level,'* by insisting that the Bank enter areas where the Bank has been reluctant to participate . . . that the Bank engage with global public goods from the perspective of the developing world.*

The CPS is also notable because it is a joint strategy between IBRD and the International Finance Corporation, which includes both private and public sector responses to GPGs, particularly on environmental commons issues. The CPS is so recent that the effectiveness of the new approach remains to be evaluated.

The Bank's attention to fostering GPGs gets diluted as it moves from corporate–level strategy down.

gies could have been more specific on how to translate corporate priorities into country-level action. Indeed, the Long-Term Strategic Exercise acknowledges the limitations of the country-based model as a tool for fostering GPGs, particularly regarding country incentives to diffuse country knowledge (World Bank 2007e).

What about the strategies "in the middle"—those of the networks[5] and Regions? A review of such documents found that explicit attention to GPGs becomes diluted as it passes from network anchor strategy to Regional strategy. And typically, neither network nor Regional strategies fully elucidate how these strategies will play out at the country level.[6] Attention to GPGs is more prominent in both network and Regional strategies dealing with the environment, as compared with those dealing with the health sector.[7] The likely reason is because of the type of intervention needed for containing communicable diseases, which requires a strong national focus that might not be explicitly connected to global action.

A good example is the Bank's environment strategy, *Making Sustainable Commitments* (World Bank 2001), and the 2007 Sector Implementation Strategy Update (World Bank 2007f), which provides a strong focus on institutions, governance, and outcomes. It is one of the few network strategies that elucidate in detail how each Bank Region should undertake actions to foster global/regional environmental commons. Translating strategy into practice, however, proved to be difficult.

The Sustainable Development Network reported in 2003 that mainstreaming environmental considerations in sectoral projects, programs, and policies had been slower than expected. IEG (2008a) found that although mainstreaming has advanced since 2001, it has remained incomplete because of limited incentives and too few independent Bank resources to integrate environmental components into other projects. The Environment

Though mainstreaming environmental considerations have advanced since 2001, it has remained incomplete due to incentives and resource limitations.

Sector Board has identified and catalyzed new partnerships for emerging climate change issues, but in other areas has not fully followed through on its stated commitments to realign global partnerships with strategic objectives and to improve the governance and management of such partnerships (IEG 2008b). Similarly, the DGF Council stated during the fiscal 2007 screening process that the environment sector "seemed to lack a unifying strategy and that proposals were not linked with country-based and other global programs" (IEG 2008b).

The Bank's Regional strategies (which vary significantly in format and vintage across Bank Regions, with Africa being particularly comprehensive) typically cover GPGs somewhat superficially. Climate change and HIV/AIDS are mentioned in all Regions, but scant attention is paid to looking at the promotion of GPGs in a more comprehensive or strategic manner. Nonetheless, some good practice is emerging in Regional and sector-specific strategies, as highlighted in box 6.2.

Box 6.2: Emerging Good Practice from the Regions

The current Latin America and Caribbean Regional strategy includes concrete references to proposed action on important GPGs. Global issues is one of the four pillars of Bank action for the Region and includes topics such as climate change, trade negotiations, HIV/AIDS, and avian flu. The Regional vice president elevated the importance of climate change and the Bank's involvement in the external media by noting in an op-ed piece that a fair global system should make lower carbon-intense emissions possible by leveling the playing field between developing and developed countries.

The 2005 Health Strategy developed by the Africa Region includes a substantive discussion of how to integrate global priorities with country priorities (World Bank 2005c). Acknowledging the growing number of global initiatives aimed at controlling communicable diseases, the document outlines the importance of the Bank in helping client countries manage and benefit from the complex array of global initiatives.

Several factors could contribute to the dilution of GPG focus in Bank strategic documents from the corporate level to the networks and Regions and finally to the country. It may be that accountability for GPG issues is lessened, or control over resources diminishes, as one moves down the management chain. Both could compromise a country team's ability and desire to advocate for and to deliver GPGs. Some interview respondents also postulate that task managers and country teams feel they have their hands full with the Bank's traditional mandate and are naturally reluctant to take on another. Without accompanying resources or accountability, a corporate mandate from above becomes more difficult to trace down to the country implementation level.

Country Programs in Practice— from Strategy to Action

In moving from strategy to action at the country level, at least three factors come into play. First, the broad attention paid by the Bank to GPGs is partly reflected in the overall allocation of corporate resources—the Bank's own budget and trust funds—to this priority. Second, the particular financial instruments at the Bank's disposal—including grants, concessional IDA, IBRD loans—influence country activities. Third, global programs have become an increasingly popular tool for the Bank to deploy. Each of these is discussed below.

Allocating the Right Level of Corporate Resources

The Bank reports that its expenditures and lending for the purposes of fostering GPGs have risen rapidly in recent years (using a widely drawn definition of GPGs, owing to the lack of specific administrative coding).[8] These estimates should be treated with some caution because they may be subject to significant variations depending on the definitions and classifications used in their construction. Indeed, going forward, more precise definition and tracking of spending would be important as management tools. Expenditures, including trust funds, have nearly doubled in five years, from $56.2 million in fiscal 2002 to $108.0 million in fiscal 2007, reaching approximately 4 percent of total Bank expenditures. The bulk of this $50 million rise is concentrated on increased spending in the GPG areas of environmental commons (an increase of $22 million) and trade (an increase of $16 million), as shown in figure 6.1.[9]

Bank expenditures are rising rapidly, with the biggest increase for work on environmental commons.

These funds come from three sources, including the Bank's core budget, Bank-executed trust

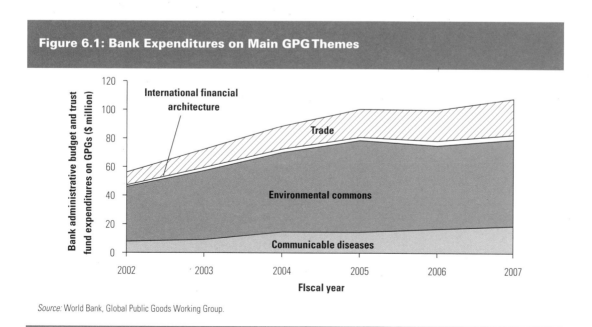

Figure 6.1: Bank Expenditures on Main GPG Themes

International financial architecture

Trade

Environmental commons

Communicable diseases

Bank administrative budget and trust fund expenditures on GPGs ($ million)

Fiscal year

Source: World Bank, Global Public Goods Working Group.

Bank lending for GPGs has more than doubled over the past five years— to about 10 percent of total lending in fiscal 2007.

funds, and other funding sources such as GEF. The core budget expenditures have nearly doubled over the period, from $32.3 million in fiscal 2002 to $59.7 million in fiscal 2007. In addition, trust fund expenditures have risen from $13.9 million to $26.2 million, and the other sources have increased from $10.1 million to $22.1 million.

IBRD and IDA lending has grown even faster, from $968 million (and 5 percent of all lending) to $2.5 billion (10 percent) over the same period. The bulk of this increase was in the area of trade, where lending volumes increased from $76 million in fiscal 2002 to $988 million in fiscal 2007 as shown in figure 6.2. A large increase also occurred in the area of environmental commons, from $467 million to $879 million. Lending for communicable diseases has fluctuated around $400 million over the period, and that for international financial architecture has been very small.

The Bank's administrative expenditure on GPGs is one of the smaller allocations for its six strategic priorities.

Other sources of funds have been prominent in financing work in environmental commons. The carbon funds, GEF, Montreal Protocol, and other special funds, together, accounted for

over $1 billion of finance in fiscal 2006 alone. While this amount was a peak, these funds accounted for an average of $270 million during fiscal 2002–07.

Are these numbers—particularly the Bank's administrative budget—adequate for the task? It is impossible to say because there is no benchmark against which to calibrate. It is possible to highlight the difficulties of budgets and incentives staff face, as reported in interviews with key respondents.[10] The budget systems of the Bank have largely been designed to fit its model of business, which has been in place for several decades—with lending as the centerpiece—and have not yet been smoothly adapted to reflect the requirements of new business. Country directors and their sector director colleagues can struggle to meet corporate pressure to conduct GPG work at the country level when there is modest or little counterpart demand and no obvious instrument for follow-up. Some innovative responses have been developed, such as the Latin America and Caribbean Region's "beam" funding, which allocates a modest share of Bank budget administrative funding on a competitive basis to Sustainable Development Network sector teams to stimulate their work on GPGs in specific countries.

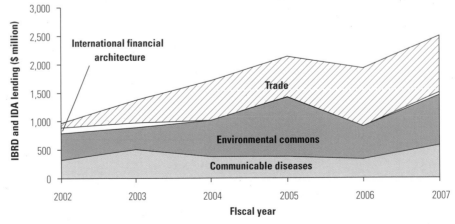

Figure 6.2: IBRD and IDA Lending for Main GPG Themes

Source: World Bank, Global Public Goods Working Group.

At the network level, staff also report that budget and incentive pressures are inhibiting, but it is difficult to assess this from an external viewpoint. The Bank's need or desire to be responsive to its shareholders and stakeholders leads it to be an active partner in a growing number of global initiatives. Network staff often do not have adequate budgets to fund their work—such as attending planning and governance meetings of global programs, or producing tailored research in response to partner requests. And against such a squeeze, the staff are placed in difficult positions of trying to fulfill other services, including providing operational and other specific support to country teams.

Overall, while the increase in resources of the Bank to GPGs has been substantial, renewed attention to those GPGs—both globally and within the Bank—implies there will be pressure for the Bank to devote substantially more emphasis and, therefore, resources to GPGs. Since the Bank's administrative budget is projected to remain flat, and across-the-board increases in lending volumes will be modest at most, the Bank would then have to rely increasingly on other sources. Grant resources and market-based mechanisms may be used to finance country-based projects, and trust funds to finance Bank expenditures. If not, the Bank would have to make a major reallocation of its own Bank budget away from its traditional work and toward GPGs.

This corporate decision to use external funding streams, particularly trust funds, to address GPGs could lead to fragmentation of efforts, rigidity over allocations, greater administrative costs, subjection to particular donor requirements and preferences, and a disconnect from the basic resource allocation mechanism that governs the country-based model. The Bank has sought to mitigate such risks through several measures, including standardizing its trust fund policies and engaging with donors to harmonize approaches.

Using Different Financing Instruments

Bank Concessional Finance—IDA

For LICs, the Bank can support country action through the concessional—and hence more attractive—financing of IDA. Indeed, in recent years, the Bank has committed substantial IDA funding to help countries in programs with clear GPG dimensions—such as HIV/AIDS, avian influenza, and environmental commons. For example, in Vietnam, the Bank has been able to use its multisectoral expertise, combined with concessional IDA finance, to help the authorities cope with the threat of avian flu, in part, because there was a strong national interest in averting economic fallout in the domestic food industry.

Often, implementation capacity on the ground is stretched, however, and in those circumstances, Bank staff report that national demands, understandably, may take precedence over some GPG considerations. Furthermore, for national counterparts who are dealing with wretched poverty or postconflict reconstruction on a day-to-day basis, the goals of GPGs can seem rather distant and lofty. Again, staff report that there is great reluctance among national partners and country teams to allow IDA allocations targeted for poverty reduction to be diverted to fostering GPGs whose benefits may not be felt by the poorest.

A related and pressing point that has been observed in several high-profile cases in Africa is the growing presence of vertical global programs and funding mechanisms. Most vertical funds are in the health sector and they focus much needed attention and resources on specific problems, such as HIV/AIDS, malaria, and other communicable diseases. While these are vital issues that pose national, regional, and sometimes global challenges, the influence of vertical funds risks diverting domestic resources from other health sector and national priorities. Such funds may place more pressure on national administrations and can exacerbate aid fragmentation.

For example, in Ethiopia, more than half of the country's health budget recently came from HIV/AIDS global programs (IEG 2005). In cases with large resources from global programs, the

Trust funds are a growing force in the delivery of GPGs—this poses challenges with regard to fragmentation, donor requirements, and preferences.

Bank must work with client countries to carefully weigh its role and comparative advantage. In doing this, there may be instances in which a track record of successful Bank support for, say, HIV/AIDS projects in a specific country warrants continuing active engagement. In other circumstances it may be better to reallocate resources away from "inundated" areas to where the Bank can be more effective, for example, in integrated health care systems. The Bank should also continue its aim to support government-led aid coordination mechanisms, and at the global level, through the Paris Declaration and follow-up measures. Progress needs to be accelerated.

IDA has innovated with special support for Regional projects. A recent innovation in IDA has been the creation of a separate funding envelope to support Regional projects. Established on a pilot basis under IDA13, the approach was continued under IDA14, and the allocation for it increased by over 70 percent under the IDA15 framework (World Bank 2008c). These resources can be used to "top-up" IDA resources provided to countries through the regular country performance-based allocation system, as applied to pertinent Regional projects. The rationale is to encourage and facilitate countries' participation in Regional projects, help defray the extra costs associated with such cross-border cooperation, and meet what is perceived to be a significant demand and opportunity for more (and more ambitious) Regional projects. The Bank's Africa Region has helped push Bank support for Regional cooperation through the creation of a director position and a dedicated unit to promote Regional projects and programs. Although it is still early, there are signs that this IDA initiative is bearing fruit. It should be monitored for lessons as to whether this approach should be replicated for some GPGs, though great care would be needed to avoid fragmenting IDA's overall framework.

Other Concessional Finance—Grants

When the Bank has an attractive instrument to support its country partners in taking action, there are signs of success. When the Bank has had a clear and viable instrument to support its country partners in taking action on some environmental concerns, there are signs of success. A good example of

this is the GEF. Formed in 1991, the GEF had a very clear mandate, with the full backing of the international community. Its basic operational structure and financial management originated in the Bank itself, and the professional experts who help promote GEF projects are Bank staff. Its grant finance has proved equally appealing to MICs and LICs alike (IEG 2007a). Indeed, in China—which has benefited from about $510 million of GEF financing in 45 projects since 1991—the presence of the GEF has been a key ingredient in helping the Bank and national authorities form a strong and practical partnership to tackle issues that would not otherwise have been addressed. Client representatives report that Bank staff have kept them adequately informed on a range of global programs and initiatives. Furthermore, Bank involvement has been valued where it helps demonstrate new approaches that can be subsequently scaled up—an important feature of China's 11th five-year plan (IEG 2007a).

In cases where the Bank has not had an obviously attractive financial instrument—and/or where there has been a lack of demand from country partners—it is less easy to see progress. For example, Bank effectiveness in promoting global environmental sustainability, including tackling climate change, has been mixed. Considerable attention has been given to biodiversity conservation, but, with the significant exception of China, less has been given to greenhouse gas mitigation, and, until recently, almost none to help countries adapt to the likely future impacts of climate change. In Senegal and Uganda, for example, the link between natural resource management and poverty has been largely overlooked in Bank lending (IEG 2008a). Much of this could be the result of a wider concern about how developing countries are compensated for their investments in GPGs. The Bank's approach is beginning to change, however, and much greater attention is envisaged by both the Bank and International Finance Corporation to climate-related challenges, including with the newly emerging Climate Investment Funds.

Several developing countries have expressed apprehension about having to design national projects that include global interests without receiving additional funding for the benefits accruing to the international community (ITF 2006). Although the inclusion of GPG concerns in national strategies is socially desirable, the issue still remains contentious about how developing countries will be compensated for having to incur higher costs (while benefits are distributed globally) when implementing development projects. For example, the creation of renewable energy electrification projects, without compensation for higher costs (as compared with traditional electrification projects), will mean a reduction in the number of beneficiaries.

Nonconcessional and Market-Based Finance

A key point reported by some operational staff and client representatives is that there is often a mismatch between country needs (and resources) and global ambitions on many GPGs.[11] In MICs, for example, the Bank tends not to be a significant player in financial terms and, indeed, its main instrument—IBRD lending—is nonconcessional (IEG 2007a). Hence the Bank's ability to influence (or persuade) a country to take concrete action on some GPGs is inherently limited, but the effective provision of those goods requires deep participation by these MICs, as discussed in box 6.3.

The limits of nonconcessional finance are illustrated in the Bank's work on avian influenza.

Only some of the benefits of controlling avian influenza can be captured by individual countries, and so it tends to remain a low national priority. So far, the Bank has supported 50 avian influenza and pandemic preparedness projects under its Global Program for Avian Influenza.[12] But only seven of these projects include IBRD finance, for a total of $94 million, and among these, only two are for sizable sums. Moreover, to date, only $12 million of IBRD loans have been disbursed.

In the two large IBRD projects—in Romania and Turkey—the positive externality of controlling avian influenza was largely captured within national borders by factors having nothing to do with the Bank. In both cases, poultry exporters were prevented from getting their products to the important European Union market because of fears that the disease could spread to people, providing strong national incentive to take quick action. This is a good example of how external pressure (economic or legal) can make the most of the Bank's country-based model for fostering certain GPGs.

In Indonesia, an evaluation of the Bank's country assistance program from 1999 to 2006 showed that it covered forestry issues with large-scale analytical work but little lending. Over that

Although the inclusion of GPGs in national strategies is desirable, doing so remains contentious.

The Bank's work on avian influenza illustrates the limits of the Bank's nonconcessional finance.

Box 6.3: Bank GPG and MIC Strategies: Fates Entwined

The provision of many GPGs depends critically on the actions of middle-income countries. Indeed, MICs are home to many of the world's most important environmental assets. They are the source of more than 40 percent of the world's carbon emissions; the strength of their financial systems directly affects the fortunes of other countries globally, and the prevention of communicable diseases by MICs could be critical to avoiding widespread contagion. Actions taken by MICs are therefore essential to the GPG agenda. Moreover, the Bank has indicated that GPGs will be a critical focus of its engagement with MICs, providing one of the primary justifications for a continuing relationship (World Bank 2006a).

In addition to these potential synergies, however, there are also tensions between these two agendas. MIC clients are increasingly calling on the Bank to become more client-focused and responsive to their needs, given the vast expansion of choice they have enjoyed in financial and technical support for development (IEG 2007a). At the same time, almost by definition, many GPGs—particularly those with the weakest link and aggregate effort characteristics—require action that countries would not otherwise choose to take. The Bank must carefully navigate these inherent tensions and trade-offs. Doing this well would lead to success and effectively deliver on both the MIC and GPG agendas, but failing on one would likely weaken the other.

period, the traction achieved by the Bank was very limited, and deforestation continued at a rapid clip.

In contrast, when national and global interests (and benefits) are closely aligned, nonconcessional finance can prove a workable instrument. Over the last two decades, the Bank has been able to secure very substantial country-based action on the promotion of trade—recognized as an important GPG. To complement its global-level work on trade regimes, the Bank has supported projects and programs in some 117 countries, with a total of $38 billion of finance (8 percent of total Bank commitments) since the late 1980s (IEG 2006a).[13] About 70 percent of those projects have delivered satisfactory development results in the countries concerned, although the poverty-reducing aspects of trade reform have not often been fully delivered (IEG 2006a). In recent years, the Bank has also creatively brought together the nexus of global, regional, and country interventions on trade—for example through successful, regionally structured, trade and transport facilitation projects (IEG 2007c).

In China, the Bank has successfully used market-based finance alongside its other, more established instruments.

The use of market-based finance, alongside other more-established instruments, is demonstrated well in the Bank's work on China, which is one of the world's largest emitters of carbon dioxide and where 70 percent of energy is coal-based. The Chinese authorities have actively engaged with the Bank, and priority has been given in the Bank's country strategies to financing clean and renewable energy as well as projects for the clean storage of carbon dioxide emissions, afforestation, and recycling. Indeed, to date the Bank's program has helped the Chinese to adopt a Renewable Energy Law, while other analytic and advisory activities and technical assistance work has focused on enhancing biodiversity. Furthermore, the Bank has been able to leverage funds from global programs like the GEF and the Multilateral Fund for the Implementation of the Montreal Protocol for renewable energy and ozone-depleting substance projects. Finally, the Bank has helped China

Global programs have grown rapidly in number.

utilize the Clean Development Mechanism of the Kyoto Protocol through carbon funds, focusing particularly on the capture of the greenhouse gas, trifluromethane.

Deploying Global Programs at the Country Level

Global and regional programs and partnerships[14] are another vehicle the Bank can use to bring national and global interests closer together. The number of these global programs supported by the Bank has grown rapidly in recent years, reaching about 160 in fiscal 2008. Global and regional programs are very diverse, in both their objectives and structure. A program can act primarily as a cross-country network, with little or no financial resources available; it can finance technical assistance; it can finance specific investments; or it can act in a combination of these ways. It can support GPGs through investments at the country, regional, or global level; or it can have nothing to do with GPGs at all.

Indeed, when one looks at the financing for these programs, three characteristics emerge. First, only 56 global programs (35 percent of the total) focus primarily on providing GPGs, as shown in figure 6.3a.[15] Second, a majority share—57 percent—of Bank-executed resources that the Bank devotes to global programs are allocated to the GPG-focused programs. Third, when one looks at all funds that the Bank manages, including recipient-executed trust funds, the share devoted to GPGs grows to a large majority, as shown in figure 6.3b—92 percent. These figures raise interesting issues regarding the prioritization of GPGs in the Bank's support for global programs.

Many global programs—particularly those that primarily deliver GPGs through national investments and technical assistance—require action at the country level. But despite the Bank's direct role as a partner in these global programs, systematic linkages to country programs have proved challenging. Many of the global programs have garnered only modest participation by MICs (IEG 2007a). And Bank performance in global programs overall has been better at the global

Figure 6.3: Most Global Programs Do Not Focus on GPGs, but Most of the Bank's GPP Resources Are Devoted to Those That Do

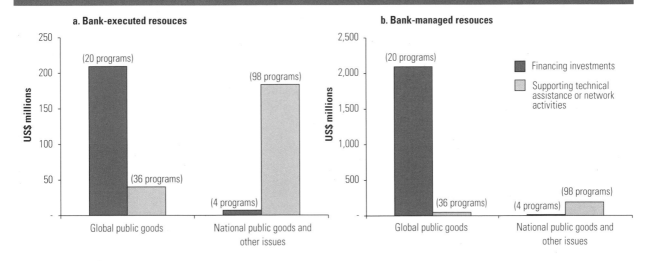

Source: World Bank database.

Note: Bank-executed resources cover Bank budget and Bank-executed trust funds. Bank-managed resources also include recipient-executed trust funds.

than at the country level, in part because, in the absence of a requirement to do so, task managers for global programs rarely demonstrate how the program will help specific countries (IEG 2004b).

One reason for limited participation by developing country partners is that the Bank's decision to support a global program can be the result of pressures beyond those coming from its client countries, including strong donor interests, advocacy by international nongovernmental organizations (NGOs), and other geopolitical considerations. Sometimes these programs attract limited interest from developing countries.

How can global programs be better integrated into country operations? Simply basing a global program within the Bank—there are 57 such programs—does not guarantee effective linkages. For example, these linkages were weak in the Population Reproductive Health Capacity Building Program, in spite of the potential synergies with Bank investment operations occurring in the same countries. Even when country teams and global program teams communicate, the natural tendency is for global

program staff and Bank staff to focus on their own activities, for which they are held accountable, while collaborating primarily with established counterparts. For example, Bank country team staff often liaise with ministry officials overseeing country programs, while global program staff often liaise with a different set of officials, donors, specific interest groups, and specialists dealing with GPGs.

Indeed, Bank Task Team Leaders of global programs have reported that there are sharp incentives against close linkages between country and global programs. On occasion, the strong presence of a global program in a country sometimes leads a country team to take a division-of-labor approach, scaling back its program in the same sector. Importantly, country teams have few resources to work on global programs unless there is a demonstrated interest by the country client. This is even more acute when a global program is housed outside the Bank because there is little or no core Bank budget earmarked for program oversight. Moreover, while country teams are interested in budget and concessional finance that may come with participation, their interest

It has proven challenging to make systematic linkages between global programs and country programs.

Merely basing a global program in the Bank does not guarantee effective linkages.

There are, in fact, strong incentives against making such linkages.

depends on the flexibility of the funding to support country priorities that may or may not overlap with global priorities.[16]

IEG has found that stronger legitimacy of a program appears to foster stronger linkages with country operations (IEG 2004b, 2008b). This legitimacy is enhanced by substantial developing-country representation in the governing body (discussed in the chapter 7). Stronger linkages emerge in the programs when developing countries have greater voice, in part because these programs are more likely to reflect developing-country interests and to be relevant to developing-country needs and circumstances.

The approach toward M&E for global and regional programs is substantially less developed than that which has been established over time for the Bank's traditional IBRD and IDA instruments. Global programs are relatively new and rarely self-sustaining financially, and hence it is very important to establish a robust M&E framework at the outset of a program. But IEG's recent review of seven global program evaluations found the quality of all seven was compromised by weak M&E systems for the program. Therefore, neither the external evaluations nor IEG found much systematic evidence relating to the achievement of the seven programs' objectives at the outcome level. It is impossible to say whether the global program interventions—together accounting for about

The approach to M&E for global programs is substantially less developed than approaches used in Bank lending.

$100 million of spending in 2007—ultimately had any effect (IEG 2008b).

The multicountry aspect of GPGs also applies to topics and responses that are best handled at the regional level, that is, by groups of neighboring countries. The Bank faces a similar challenge in demonstrating how it can link regional and country concerns and opportunities. One major instrument for doing this is through regional programs, which have increased in importance in recent years, though they still account for a modest share of Bank lending. In reviewing CASs, it is clear that mentioning regional programs is also much more the exception than the rule.

As the cross-border dimensions of health, environment, and trade facilitation are expanding worldwide, the contribution of regional programs to address regional public goods and GPGs is likely to grow in significance. Consensus among participating countries regarding the distribution of program benefits and costs, as well as strong country voice in governance arrangements, are key characteristics which IEG identified in successful regional programs (IEG 2007c). An example of an effective regional program is the Regional Hydropower Development Project, which was designed to manage the Senegal River Basin serving Mali, Mauritania, and Senegal. This project built a hydroelectric plant that successfully responded to the needs of the three countries by providing a reliable, low-cost power supply and increased electricity access.

Chapter 7

Evaluation Highlights

- Bank advocacy goes beyond the country level and involves producing collective global responses and promoting the development interests of the poor.
- Promoting global trade reform represents the Bank's advocacy at its best—in its analytical and practical depth and its proactive dissemination.
- The Bank's advocacy work on avian influenza built on robust economic analysis, convening power, fiduciary reputation, and multisectoral expertise.
- The Bank has had some advocacy successes related to environmental commons, though its influence on advancing work on climate change is more debatable.
- The voice of developing countries is still underrepresented in global programs, particularly in their governance.

Indonesian elementary schoolchildren wear surgical masks in response to 2003 outbreak of SARS in China; photo ©Reuters/ Corbis, reproduced by permission.

The Bank's Advocacy on Global Public Goods: What Has Worked and What Has Not?

The Dimensions of Advocacy

The Bank can advocate for action on GPGs in at least three ways. First, it can encourage specific actions supported by the global community at the country level. This lies at the heart of the Bank's country-based model and was discussed in chapter 6.

Second, the Bank can help inform collective global responses to providing GPGs. For example, independent and robust research on the costs of communicable disease threats (such as avian flu) can help inform international partners in developing an appropriate response. Practical analysis, and sometimes the Bank's convening power, can also be used to help develop markets—such as that for carbon finance—and so deliver new tools to provide GPGs.

Third, the Bank's focus on poverty and development can be used to promote the interests of developing countries in international dialogue on mechanisms to tackle GPG issues. This is particularly applicable where the community of nations considers developing and implementing (binding) international agreements to set a framework for collective action. In such cases, the Bank has a potentially powerful ability to ensure that development interests are properly considered—not least, how costs and benefits

of new arrangements will affect the world's poor.

This chapter explains aspects of advocacy using three high-profile examples—trade, environmental commons, and avian influenza. It draws on the importance of voice for developing countries, especially related to the governance of global programs. Finally, it presents a perspective on very recent innovations of the Bank in supporting advocacy through its financial capabilities.

Advocacy at Its Best: The Bank's Experience with Trade

The role of the Bank as a constructive advocate for developing countries on GPG issues has been shown in its work on trade (IEG 2006a). Arguably, the Bank was somewhat slow to emphasize this strand of its work, but it was given prominence from 2001 onward, significantly later than other country-based components of the Bank's work which had been growing since the late 1980s. But the Bank emerged as a leader in global trade work with high-profile reports ahead of major international trade reform meetings in Doha (2002) and Cancun (2004).[1]

Furthermore, the Bank's advocacy role was useful in positioning the Bank among client countries, especially those with which it might otherwise be less engaged on trade issues. For instance, even though some Latin America countries had been skeptical with regard to the Bank's policy advice because of the perceived failure of the Washington Consensus (Rodrik 2006), the Bank has had an active country-level engagement on trade. This illustrates an important connection—that the Bank may indeed have to be seen as a constructive advocate in the global arena if it is to open doors at the country level, to persuade and work with national partners to deliver on-the-ground action. It may well be that on other GPG priorities—for example, climate change—the Bank is not yet seen as such a high-profile advocate for developing countries, hence constraining its delivery capacity at the country level.

Key ingredients included a long period of working directly with partner countries, first-rate research capacity, and a willingness to engage in public debate.

What were the ingredients that contributed to the Bank's advocacy role in trade? Certainly a long gestation period of working on the ground and directly with partner countries (especially through the late 1980s and into the 1990s) on trade issues, gave the Bank a good understanding of, and motivation to promote, the impact of trade on development. This was a case in which the global-country link worked in both directions.

Beyond that, the assembly in-house of first-rate intellectual and analytical research capacity on trade was essential (Deaton and others 2006).[2] This gave the platform for the Bank to produce detailed, innovative, and well-regarded reports that informed the ongoing debate in trade, most notably the benefits to be gained from a more free-market approach to the markets for agricultural products and other

The Bank's work also gained traction in the context of "live" negotiations for the Doha round of trade talks.

items produced in significant quantities in the developing world. The research itself was accompanied by a proactive and highly visible dissemination effort. One aspect was a willingness to engage in public debate—including in mainstream media channels—and take what some might regard as fairly strong positions on issues of some contentiousness.[3] All of this took place in a very specific setting: the live negotiations for the Doha round of the World Trade Organization rules-based regime. This last point is also critical, because it gave the Bank's work a direct opportunity to gain traction.

The advocacy role was not an unqualified success, and at least two drawbacks have appeared. Recently, the analytical basis and findings of some of the Bank's earlier work has been challenged, and indeed some recalibrations have been made. This, in itself, hardly undoes the impact of the Bank's advocacy but it illustrates the difficulty of putting in place analytical foundations that are deep and can stand the test of time. The second drawback relates to how advocacy is then followed through with practical action to build developing-country capacity. The most high-profile initiative in trade capacity-building work was the Bank's involvement in the Integrated Framework for Trade-Related Technical Assistance—a multidonor, multiagency collaboration set up in 1997 to provide trade-related technical assistance to 49 less-developed countries. This global program instrument exhibited some weaknesses, however, including a slow pace of implementation, insufficient focus on improved trade outcomes, and a shortage of funds. The absence of a good results-based management framework also typifies a problem common to a good number of global programs.

The Complex Challenge of Environmental Commons and Climate Change

The Bank has long paid attention to the global dimension of the environmental commons—and more recently to climate change itself. Indeed, there are very specific examples in which the Bank has played a practical advocacy role to develop new approaches to what is a very complex challenge. When the GEF was being put together, there was considerable debate among partners as to whether resources should be new or drawn from existing allocations to the Bank (and others). For its part, the Bank did play an advocacy role and is reported as holding the position that "it would participate only if additional funding was made available." In the end, an agreement was reached in London in 1990 with "the World Bank, and specifically the president of the bank, clearly designated as the administrator and manager of the central function of the fund: financing projects and programs to meet the incremental costs of article 5 [that is, developing country] parties" (Benedick 1998).

The Prototype Carbon Fund (PCF) emerged from advocacy work by the Bank and others, as explained in box 7.1. The main, universally recognized contribution of the PCF is that it gave credibility to the burgeoning field of carbon finance. The PCF is also respected by several experts in the field because they assess the methodologies it has developed for ascertaining additionality to be relatively sound, especially as compared with other projects approved by the United Nations Clean Development Mechanism. Some 22 methodologies for measuring additionality developed in the PCF and Carbon Finance Unit of the Bank have been approved by the Clean Development Mechanism. But there is not unanimity on these issues, as shown in box 7.1.

Advocacy has also been very noticeable in the Bank's contribution to setting up new Climate Investment Funds. Emerging from preliminary high-level discussions at the Gleneagles Summit in 2005, the creation of these funds has been assisted by the Bank and other partners over the last three years. Now it is reported that a multibillion dollar pledge has been made by the governments of Japan, the United Kingdom, and the

On environmental commons, the Bank has played a positive advocacy role in some very practical settings.

Box 7.1: Advocacy for Carbon Finance: The Bank's Role in the Growth of a World Market

Since the 1990s, the Bank has supported proposals for carbon finance—an instrument to contain carbon dioxide and other harmful emissions by allowing a developed country government or company to meet some of its own environmental obligations by investing in projects in developing countries, to help reduce emissions there. The Bank's president promulgated the concept at the United Nations General Assembly in 1997 (World Bank 1997), and the Bank's advocacy bore fruit with the launch of the Prototype Carbon Fund in 2000, the world's first carbon fund. Since then, the PCF's catalytic effect has been an example of advocacy through demonstration, and has been one factor in the global carbon market's exponential growth, from $38 million in 2002, to $64,000 million in 2007.

Carbon finance is not without controversy, and critics have questioned the extent to which additionality occurs and if invested projects are truly sustainable. For example, two studies by outside observers conclude that "additionality is unlikely or questionable for up to 40 percent of registered projects" and that "left to market forces, the Clean Development Mechanism does not significantly contribute to sustainable development." A forthcoming detailed IEG examination of additionality in Bank-supported carbon projects should give a more accurate assessment.

The PCF's advocacy position was initially hampered around the issue of governance. The host developing countries had no voice in PCF governance. In response to this situation, the Bank, after the first year of PCF operation, created a Host Country Committee, which now covers all Bank-managed carbon funds. But the Host Country Committee remains strictly advisory and some members still complain that they have no contact with the funds' participants committees.[a] Other members and Bank managers argue that some aspects of the operational structure cannot be fully inclusive because of the need to discuss confidential pricing information. Some Host Country Committee members would like to see in-country capacity-building efforts on a greater scale and impact than the $21 million allocated to the Carbon Finance Assist program, housed in the World Bank Institute.

The new Carbon Partnership Facility, scheduled to become operational later in 2008, will need to carefully address these and other tensions.

a. The two committees meet at the same time but in different rooms. The current Chair of the PCF Participants Committee has never met the Chair of the Host Country Committee. Under the new Bank-supported Carbon Partnership Facility, expected to become operational in late 2008, host-country members are to have equal representation and voting rights with company members.

United States to kick-start this significant initiative. But as illustrated in box 7.2, there is substantial pressure on the Bank to mainstream climate-friendly approaches into all its development work.

The example of the Montreal Protocol (and indeed of the carbon finance business, which emerged from the incentives created by Kyoto Protocol commitments) illustrates an important point: the World Bank can play a strong role in the supply of GPGs, but primarily when supported by an appropriate treaty instrument. The Montreal Protocol is one of the most successful treaties in history. The Bank has contributed to its success, but the real credit belongs to the treaty itself and to the nature of this particular global challenge (Barrett, 2008). Similarly, the Bank's ability to contribute to the much harder problem of climate change will depend on the effectiveness of the treaty arrangement for this challenge.

The extent to which the Bank has been a leading influential advocate on climate change is more debatable.

The extent to which the Bank has been a leading advocate to date on the broad issue of climate change is more debatable, particularly now that global climate change is considered by many as one of the greatest challenges of our time. The Bank's analytical and research work has certainly been less prominent in this sphere than in the trade arena. While major publications such as the Stern report, and the advocacy of Nobel Prize winners, have been recognized worldwide, the Bank's materials have neither been as hard-hitting nor attracted the same level of attention. This may be because the Bank's need to balance different viewpoints among its shareholders has constrained its room to maneuver. It may reflect a less-than-strong skill set to produce the necessary leading research, as suggested in IEG's environment evaluation (2008a). Or perhaps at this stage of the cycle, the Bank is only now (appropriately) beginning to gear up on the advocacy front.

Whatever the mix of factors in the explanation, it is becoming ever more pressing for the Bank to approach the advocacy element of climate change (and its important dimension on development) more visibly and forcefully. The Bank president's public statements,[4] and the opportunity opened by the new Strategic Framework for Climate Change, provide a platform upon which to build.

One important area in which the Bank's advocacy can be ramped up relates to the adapta-

---

Box 7.2: Clean and Dirty Energy—Can the Bank Do Both?

Some external commentators criticize the Bank Group, arguing that while it is doing the right thing in expanding its climate-friendly initiatives—through GEF projects, the creation of the Prototype Carbon Fund, and some analytical research—it is doing the wrong thing by continuing to finance large energy and infrastructure projects that emit carbon dioxide on a massive scale (Wheeler 2008).

Withdrawing from or reducing investments in traditional projects would be a major challenge. As recently as fiscal 2006, these energy investments accounted for 92 percent of the Bank's total energy portfolio, or nearly $2 billion (World Bank 2007g). And there continues to be equally substantial pipeline demand. It is argued that these investments are meeting a real development need, and one cannot expect such a transformational "sea change" to occur overnight (House of Commons 2008). Moreover, some critics argue the Bank has little incentive to scale down a line of business that, particularly in IBRD countries, provides a steady flow of profitable projects in the context of declining lending volumes (Redman 2008).

Can the seeming contradiction be reconciled? There are steps the Bank Group can take. One would be to include a shadow price for carbon emissions in project appraisals, and to set a timetable for its introduction as a key factor in decision making by, say, 2010. Another would be to start costing out and regularly reporting on the subsidy that would be required in any given year to help these energy and infrastructure projects become climate-friendly. This would provide the international community with better ongoing knowledge of the price tab for collective action, and how far it is being met.

tion to climate change. Adaptation is needed because of the failure (to date primarily by industrialized countries) to supply the GPG of climate change mitigation. IEG's evaluations have argued that the Bank could be strategic and effective with regard to reducing the vulnerability of countries and the poor to natural disasters and climate change (IEG 2008a). They also concluded that the Bank Group has not been able to provide financial resources to assist countries to address environmental concerns as high priorities. The emphasis in the IDA15 replenishment on the Bank's role in assisting eligible countries to adapt to climate change is a step forward in this regard.

The industrialized countries have acknowledged a responsibility to assist poor countries in adapting to climate change. What they have not determined is, first, a basis for calculating this assistance and, second, an arrangement for determining burden-sharing among the industrialized countries. The World Bank can help in calculating the level of financial support needed and then in implementing an adaptation assistance program. Indeed, the connection between adaptation and development is so intimate that the Bank is arguably the only global institution capable of playing this role.

Another angle on which advocacy could be enhanced relates to research and technology capability to produce climate-friendly solutions in many areas—including transport and energy production—suited for developing countries. Most attention has focused on the need for research and development (R&D) to be undertaken by the industrialized countries, with the technologies embodying this new knowledge being transferred to developing countries.[5] However, technologies appropriate for industrialized countries may be less so for developing countries, given the different contexts. New technologies may be needed but currently this kind of R&D is seen to be somewhat neglected.

Developing countries need to be able to determine which technologies are necessary, whether the technologies available have to be adapted to suit local circumstances, and how these technologies should be deployed and used. All of this requires a robust technical and scientific capability. This links to another of the Bank's strategic priorities—engaging with MICs, including Brazil, China, India, and Russia. This strategy is essential if the Bank is to play a meaningful role in helping the development transformation needed to mitigate climate change. Technology R&D is also needed for the world's poorest countries, but for reasons of scale, a policy that focuses exclusively on this latter group of countries would be unlikely to properly address the mitigation challenge.

It is becoming ever more pressing for the Bank to advocate for development interests in climate change more visibly and forcefully.

Such an advocacy position is consistent with that put forward by the International Task Force on Global Public Goods (ITF 2006), an exercise led by respected developing country leaders, practitioners, and opinion makers. It recommended establishing an International Consultative Group on Clean Energy Research, "which includes both developed and developing countries, to collaborate and exchange information on research and development of more efficient and cleaner technologies." The recent report by the Global Leadership for Climate Action (GLCA 2007) endorses this idea. These proposals draw inspiration from the Consultative Group on International Agricultural Research (CGIAR)—a network to which the World Bank is tightly connected.

Other opportunities for advocacy include promoting research and development tailored for the developing world.

Climate change adaptation will also require innovation in other areas. A key area for future innovation might be called climate-resilient agriculture, a need which CGIAR has recognized. World Bank research has also begun to show the effects of climate change on agriculture.[6]

Creating a Unified Response: Learning from Avian Flu

The World Bank is seen by some partners to be playing an important role in the global response to threats emerging from avian flu and a potential human pandemic influenza. In terms of global

The Bank has advocated for global action on avian flu.

action, the Bank identifies its comparative advantages as coordinating global responses and mobilizing finance, and thus far it has been quite an effective advocate along those dimensions.

The Bank's leadership role in coordinating a global response to avian and human influenza—beyond what is typically expected of a financial institution—has been seen as critical.[7] Its early analysis of the global costs to the spread of avian influenza and the threat of a global pandemic (Brahmbhatt 2005) provided an umbrella under which the international technical agencies and the United Nations System Influenza Coordinator and donors could operate. This work identified the control of avian and human influenza as a GPG, noted its urgency, and helped bring global attention to the issue.

Given the urgency of this threat, the Bank helped quickly to convene major global partners around a strategy for action. Along with the World Health Organization, Food and Agricultural Organization, and World Organization for Animal Health, the Bank sponsored the first large-scale international meeting on the topic in Geneva in November 2005. The meeting was attended by more than 600 experts from over 100 countries, with substantial high-level government participation.

According to high-level participants, the Bank made several contributions at these meetings. First, it convinced international partners of the importance of integrated country plans that take into account animal health, human health, and pandemic preparedness. This was important because the Bank was the only sponsoring organization with a multisector perspective, without prejudice toward intervention in one sector over another. Second, the Bank argued that a global program should benefit developing countries, given that the response would have to be delivered on a country level and country-owned initiatives have proven to be most effective. Third, it helped to keep focus on developing the implementation arrangements for a global program

Important ingredients included the Bank's robust economic analysis, convening power, fiduciary reputation, and multisectoral expertise and orientation.

that could operate effectively, and an agreement of this type was reached during the run-up to and including the Geneva conference.

Close collaboration with other major international organizations, with each working to its comparative advantage, was essential in the response to avian flu. There have not been any major conflicts between the Bank and the relevant UN agencies on avian flu. Some counterparts have expressed concern in IEG interviews, however, that the Bank may have gone a bit beyond its comparative advantage (to arrange finance for the technical strategies of the World Health Organization, Food and Agricultural Organization, and World Organization for Animal Health) and taken a more wide-ranging role that considered technical agencies as inputs. Others have been critical that the international community's collaboration has a weak spot in underestimating the severe global economic costs—both direct and indirect—that are likely in the event of a pandemic (Osterholm 2007). Overall, this experience illustrates a wider point about the importance of collaboration among international agencies, also pertinent to the Bank's advocacy position on HIV/AIDS, as described in box 7.3.

The Bank also supported efforts to mobilize finance to address avian and human influenza, particularly with regard to the "nuts and bolts" aspects of the challenge. The Bank's research into the possible global economic impact of a pandemic influenza that might be the result of uncontrolled avian influenza, noted above, found that the ultimate costs to the world economy could be several percentage points of gross domestic product (Brahmbhatt 2005). More recent research has put the price tag at $2 trillion, and economic (but not human) costs would be concentrated among the wealthy countries. This revealed to developed nations the potential costs of inaction. The Bank also estimated country-by-country financing needs to control avian influenza and delay or reduce the probability of a pandemic (World Bank 2006b). This created a baseline against which to measure pledges, commitments, and disbursements.

> ## Box 7.3: Importance of Collaboration on Advocacy: HIV/AIDS
>
> The Bank's work on HIV/AIDS stepped up considerably in the late 1990s after internal pressure from the health sector staff in Bank Regions and the Research Department, and externally from newly created international agencies such as UNAIDS. The Bank then proactively raised awareness and demand for HIV/AIDS support among its staff and client countries.
>
> The collaboration with civil society also ultimately influenced HIV/AIDS advocacy within the Bank on other important global health issues. International NGOs worked with developing country partners to spearhead a global campaign to make existing drugs for HIV/AIDS and other diseases affordable to the populations of developing countries. They lobbied for preferential pricing for drugs and drug donations to developing countries. They supported developing countries in the potential to exercise their rights under international trade and intellectual property rights agreements. While the Bank and World Health Organization were slow to take a position on these issues, they have come to support wider access to drugs (IEG 2004b).

Working with the European Commission and other partners, the Bank helped prompt donors to pledge $1.8 billion (well above the $1.2 billion target) at an early 2006 conference in Beijing. Since that time, there has not been an outbreak of a pandemic, media attention has receded, and the topic may be seen as less urgent. Although an additional $900 million was pledged at later conferences in Bamako and New Delhi, the amount was below the financing needs identified on those occasions.

The Bank and United Nations System Influenza Coordinator have since worked closely to monitor commitments and disbursements of funds pledged at the three conferences, and to encourage donors to follow through on their commitments. Thus far, resources actually committed have not kept up with existing financing gaps (UNSIC and World Bank 2007). And while the international partners agreed that integrated country plans were the key platform from which to tackle avian flu—and would involve activities for which very significant resources would be needed—only 40 percent of committed funds have been allocated to these plans. Furthermore, as shown in figure 7.1, of those $700 million of funds committed to country programs so far, less than half have been disbursed, a much lower share than for funds committed to international or regional banks.[8] This has left a gap in the finances available in many poorer countries, particularly in Africa, to tackle this global challenge. Perhaps this difficulty could have been ameliorated either with better coordination among donor partners or with a centralized funding mechanism dedicated to actions in developing countries.

Effective Advocacy Benefits from Voice and Representation

To be an effective advocate, the programs the Bank supports must be seen to be legitimate. But the voice of developing countries in GPG arenas—not least in the governance of many global programs—is still underrepresented, and the question remains as to whether the Bank could have pushed harder to rectify this imbalance. While the organizational and strategic settings of such global programs vary, they share the common feature that they need to promote the cooperation and collective action of their own members to be effective. This puts the emphasis squarely on how to promote the participation of developing countries, which are among the intended beneficiaries of global programs and without whose engagement the effectiveness of many such programs may not be assured (Woods, forthcoming).

Giving proper voice and representation in global programs improves their responsiveness and long-term sustainability.

There is not, however, a single best-practice governance framework for global programs because they differ markedly in size and scope and employ a diverse array of governance

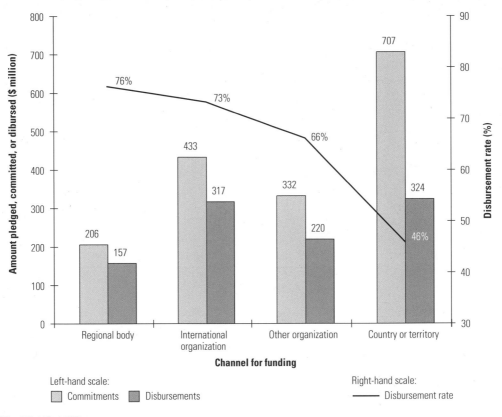

Figure 7.1: Less Than Half of Funds Committed to Integrated Country Plans Have Been Disbursed

Source: UNSIC and World Bank 2007.

Note: Approximately $650 million of pledged funds have yet to be committed to specific countries, projects, or programs.

models associated with the history and culture of each program (see box 7.4 for an example). IEG has emphasized the need for a global program "to establish legitimacy on a basis other than shareholder rights," pointing to the value of adopting an inclusive and participatory governance framework (IEG 2007b). It can take considerable time and effort by partners and the Bank to develop good governance arrangements at the start-up of a global or regional program—but this is time well spent.

Governance arrangements in several programs—including the GEF and CGIAR—have improved over time. The evidence from important programs bears this out. In the case of the regional programs for Central Asia biodiversity and for the West Africa HIV/AIDS project, it took about two years to reach agreements among the participants on the appropriate institutional

and governance structure. But that was time the stakeholders considered a good investment, in light of the inclusiveness of the governance arrangements on which they were able to agree (IEG 2007c). It paid off because the structures were able to help resolve ongoing differences and sustain the buy-in of participants. And a far bigger global program—the GEF—took a considerable degree of institutional experimentation to achieve a governance framework that is currently regarded by many as participatory and inclusive, as noted in box 7.4.

Nonetheless, there is often a tension—actual or perceived—between organizational efficiency (which may be fostered by streamlined governance arrangements) and voice. While in many programs, developing countries are represented in the governing bodies, "stake-

---

Box 7.4: Governance as Institutional Experimentation: GEF

The GEF began as a pilot program in 1991, with 16 OECD members and 9 developing countries pledging resources and representing the sole form of governance. Subsequently, the move from a pilot to a more established program resulted in a governance structure that melds those of the United Nations and the World Bank. Governance is based on a constituency system that allows for "a relatively small and effective Board," instead of the "one-country, one-seat, and one-vote system in the United Nations General Assembly," while maintaining the potential for universal representation (Woods and Lombardi 2006).

The more balanced representation of developing countries—through 18 of the 32 constituencies—is enhanced by the double-majority voting rule. When decisions are not supported by a consensus, they must garner the formal votes of at least a 60 per-

cent majority of the total number of participants in the GEF, as well as of a majority representing 60 percent of total contributions to the facility. Another feature supporting a greater sense of ownership of developing countries over the GEF is that the council cochairperson—in addition to the permanent cochairperson position provided by the chief executive—rotates between developed and developing countries.

The GEF governance also provides an institutionalized setting for engaging NGOs—a crucial factor in enhancing country-level coordination and country ownership. Participation by NGOs, both local and international, does not only take place at the project level but also at the policy-making level. GEF provides observer status for NGOs at council meetings and holds consultations with them in conjunction with each council meeting.

---

holder and shareholder influence is not always balanced," and "donors and international agencies still largely govern the programs" (IEG 2004b). In some cases, the increase in representation in the main governing body has created problems of organizational efficiency. But governance arrangements need not be static, and the changes in the CGIAR (highlighted in box 7.5) illustrate how adjustments and compromises can be made. Likewise, the Association for the Development of Education in Africa has recently decided to establish an executive committee and Cities Alliance has transformed its former steering committee into an executive body (IEG 2008b).

The emphasis in the current debate on fostering public goods raises the issue of the extent to which MICs are appropriately engaged in the governance of relevant global programs. The Bank itself has indicated that "a promising aspect of its relationship with MICs lies in its role in making connections between these partner countries and the provision of global public goods" (World Bank 2006a). Yet insufficient voice in global program governance is still a concern

---

Box 7.5: From Shareholder to Stakeholder Model: CGIAR

CGIAR, founded in 1971 and jointly sponsored by the World Bank, Food and Agriculture Organization, International Fund for Agricultural Development, andUnited Nations Development Programme, has grown from an informal small club of donors with a shared concern for agricultural research into a partnership that now includes 25 developing and 22 industrialized countries, 4 private foundations, 13 regional and international organizations, which provide financing, technical, and strategic support to a network of 15 research centers, mostly located in developing countries.

The expansion of the membership, the widening of the research agenda, and the collective-action problems arising from the grow-

ing number of centers and donors, led CGIAR to establish an executive council, with the aim of simplifying the network's decision making. Following the recommendations of the Change Design and Management Team, in 2001, the council was set up as a stakeholder body appointed by CGIAR members to follow up on the group's decisions, to ensure alignment and congruence of recommendations, and to act on decisions requiring a more urgent time frame than the schedule of the group's Annual General Meeting would allow.

The establishment of the council, with formally elected members accountable to the particular groups they represent, was needed to increase the legitimacy as well as the efficiency of CGIAR.

for MICs, inhibiting their enthusiasm for and engagement in such programs (IEG 2007a). Even the larger MICs are represented in the decision-making bodies of only a small fraction of global programs, while, in contrast, several high-income countries are included in the governance of a much larger number.

Governance arrangements for global programs can change over time. The governance arrangements for any specific global program—and how its advocacy position then emerges over time—are the results of many influences. The Bank is but one of those influences and hence responsibility for success or failure cannot rest solely—or perhaps even primarily—at its door. Indeed, the Bank's position is complex, and in a program it can play up to 11 different roles including that of convener and trust-fund manager.[9] But that multiplicity of roles creates tensions and, indeed, potential for conflicts of interest (such as that between being a funder and a beneficiary), which must be carefully managed.

Moving forward, the growing involvement of the Bank in the provision of GPGs is associated with its own governance framework. Good governance is essential to help the Bank shape its broader strategy for GPGs, define and be selective in its own role in global programs, manage potential or actual conflicts of interests arising from the various global programs, and enhance its role as an advocate for developing-country needs. Alternatively, there is a risk that "strategies will be hard to define, legitimacy will suffer, and implementation will lag" (ITF 2006).

The experience of some global programs is quite encouraging in certain respects. Once all the stakeholders acknowledged the dynamic nature of a program's governance, they *The Bank's financial robustness and reputation can be put to good use through innovative financial instruments that help move advocacy to action.* embarked on a reform process through which considerable changes have been introduced to the governance framework. Far from impairing the overall effectiveness of the program itself, this has prompted wider engagement of developing countries, resulting in greater effectiveness for the overall program. This reinforces the Bank Development Committee's own underscoring of "the importance of enhancing voice and participation [in the Bank] for all developing and transition countries" through an "inclusive and consultative" process among shareholders.[10]

New Dimensions of Advocacy: Innovation through Financial Capabilities

The creativity and innovation of the Bank has been displayed in its work to leverage funds for innovative approaches to development, especially applied to GPG challenges. The International Financing Facility for Vaccines and Immunization (IFFIm) provides an example. IFFIm sought to find a way for the international community to increase resources for life-saving vaccines and health services in developing countries. Its solution is to borrow from the international capital markets, based on donors' firm medium-term commitments, and then delivering that finance quickly and predictably through the Global Alliance for Vaccines and Immunization.

The Bank can hardly be said to have played an explicit, traditional advocacy role in proposing and developing the concept of IFFIm. Rather, the original idea was formulated in a proposal by the United Kingdom's government, with the support of other interested parties, including the Bill and Melinda Gates Foundation. But the Bank has played an important role in using its financial capabilities and reputation in moving this advocacy to action. Specifically, at the request of IFFIm, the Bank has a range of treasury management and related services, which has gotten IFFIm off the ground. The Bank, in effect, acted as the start-up treasurer for this global initiative, and deployed creative approaches with prudent fiduciary standards in the international capital markets. It raised nearly US$1 billion through a bond issue in November 2006, almost all the proceeds of which Global Alliance for Vaccines and Immunization scheduled to spend on immunization and health programs in poor countries through 2007. The initiative is still young and it will be important to assess the extent to

THE BANK'S ADVOCACY ON GLOBAL PUBLIC GOODS: WHAT HAS WORKED AND WHAT HAS NOT?

69

which IFFIm delivers additional financing over the long run.

Another innovative approach is the advanced market commitment for vaccines, also aimed at tackling communicable diseases on a global scale. Again, it would not appear that the Bank was a prime mover in the genesis of the proposal, and hence the potential for it to play a first-mover advocacy role was not captured. But the Bank's technical expertise and reputation for financial soundness has been called upon by partners to move this advocacy to action. The Bank has contributed to an international advisory group and independent expert committee that has worked on the technical and structural options for a pilot advance market commitment, and proposed that such a commitment target pneumococcal diseased as the first problem and conduct subsequent work on malaria.

Chapter 8

Bengal tiger; photo ©DLILLC/Corbis, reproduced by permission.

Improving the Bank's Support for Global Public Goods: Lessons from Experience

The Bank's country-based model works well in fostering GPGs when there is one (and preferably more) of the following: (a) a reasonable convergence at the country level of national and global interests and time horizons for taking action; (b) a dedicated cadre of staff with credible technical and managerial competence to advance specific GPG concerns; and/or (c) grant finance to provide the right incentives for action.

So the country model has its place, but these features are not always present. Where they cannot be established, a very significant shift in the country-based model is needed for the Bank to find a way to bridge the gap even more effectively between global needs and country preferences.

Indeed, looking ahead, the great shared global challenges are increasingly those where national and global benefits—actual or perceived, immediate or for the next generation—diverge significantly from each other. For example, the investments needed to protect the earth's climate and environmental commons vary considerably at local, national, and global levels, as do the costs and benefits of such actions. There are lessons emerging from this review that suggest effective measures in five areas that may help the Bank upgrade its ability to foster GPGs and to bridge the gap between global needs and country concerns more effectively.

First, the Bank can create better incentives to deliver GPGs effectively at the country level. This will include new approaches to setting budgets and recognizing the performance of managers and staff. On budget setting, one option is to set aside significant administrative funding at the corporate level to be allocated—transparently and perhaps competitively—to high-priority GPG work at the country level. Care would be needed to make sure such funding was used as a genuine addition by country teams and not simply to displace other activity. To provide better incentives to staff, managers at all levels should consider recognizing country- and global-level work on GPGs in performance management systems.

Second, the Bank can consider clearer organizational arrangements to best select, and indeed link together, responses at country, regional, and global levels. Some Regions may want to have a dedicated staff resource advancing work on regional programs (and regional public goods), as has been done in Africa, and perhaps expand their purview to cover GPGs as well. But this is not a one-size-fits-all prescription, and other Regions may have different arrangements suitable to their circumstances.

Third, a more effective approach to the delivery of the Bank's global knowledge and capacity to country teams working on GPGs would be beneficial. To this end, the way the Bank can best deploy its expertise, particularly that of its specialists located at the center of the institution in the network anchors, should be reviewed.

Fourth, the Bank and its stakeholders could renew attention toward ensuring that the perspective of developing countries is connected effectively with global responses. The Bank might be able to use its standing more powerfully to give greater voice to developing countries in the governance of significant global programs. It should take a more proactive stance in advocating for development interests—and developing country partners—in international forums (and agreements) dealing with GPGs. That would include the Bank continuing to secure additional development assistance and to promote the design and use of market-based instruments to help developing countries provide GPGs. The Bank could also explore further ways to stimulate South-South exchange of knowledge—and the development and application of new technologies designed with and for the South—on contributing to GPGs, such as climate-friendly energy production and use.

Finally, a firmer and more precise justification is needed for the costs and benefits of actions being proposed for the Bank's work on fostering GPGs, to ensure that such work is financially and institutionally sustainable over the long term. Particularly for global programs, the Bank must redouble its efforts to be more selective in its engagement and more forthright in exiting those programs whose benefits and cost-effectiveness are questionable. The Bank should also be insistent about putting in place, and using, sound results frameworks, underpinned by realistic and cost-effective monitoring and evaluation systems.

Appendixes

APPENDIX A: PROJECT PERFORMANCE RESULTS

This appendix presents long-term trends in project performance, based on IEG project evaluations using the year 1990 as a starting point and with data up until June 16, 2008. The analysis of the Bank's lending effectiveness focuses on IEG's key performance criteria: the development outcome of projects.

Performance Trends

Outcome

Seventy-six percent of projects (by number) in exit fiscal 2007 were rated moderately satisfactory or better, as shown in figure A.1, just about meeting the Strategic Compact target of 75 percent. But this was a sharp decline of 7 percentage points in performance from 83 percent in fiscal 2006. Project performance also declined when weighted by the value of disbursements, from 90 percent in fiscal 2006, to 83 percent in fiscal 2007.

How much do the results of fiscal 2007 affect the three-year rolling average of the Bank's project performance? In the medium term, lending outcomes were satisfactory—in the three years up to end-fiscal 2007, 80 percent of projects satisfactorily delivered their targeted results, up from around 70 percent at the start of the decade, as shown in figure A.2. But the three-year average, which had increased every year since 1999, except for a small dip in fiscal 2003, was flat in 2007 because of the weak fiscal 2007 cohort.

Figure A.1: Project Performance Improves in FY06, But FY07's Cohort Declines

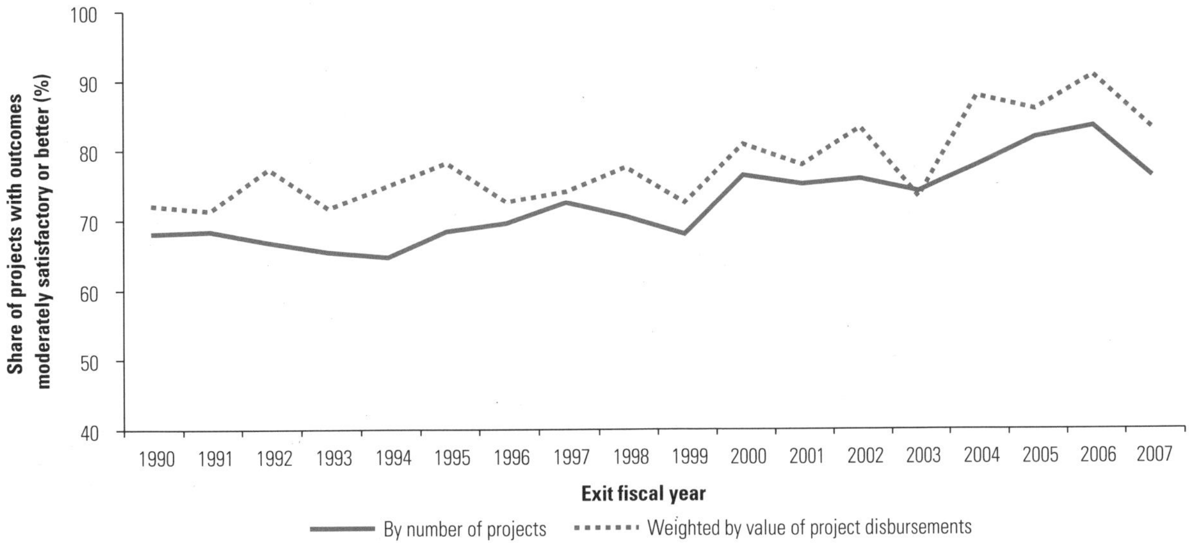

Source: World Bank database.

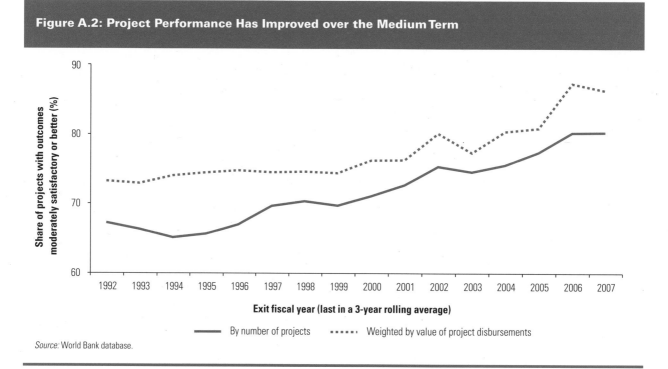

Figure A.2: Project Performance Has Improved over the Medium Term

Share of projects with outcomes moderately satisfactory or better (%)

Exit fiscal year (last in a 3-year rolling average)

—— By number of projects   ∙∙∙∙∙ Weighted by value of project disbursements

Source: World Bank database.

What drove the fiscal 2007 decline? Sometimes, a difference in the performance of the Bank's portfolio from one year to the next can be influenced by a change in the composition of projects being evaluated—for example, if there is a larger share of projects in challenging sectors or countries. But the change in portfolio composition in fiscal 2007 from the previous three years—related to Region, sector, instrument, lending arm, proportion of loans to conflict-affected countries, and other factors—does not explain the fall in ratings. Indeed, the fiscal 2007 composition of projects was actually favorable along several dimensions.

For instance, even if the fiscal 2007 cohort had maintained the same composition of adjustment and investment loans as in fiscal 2004–06, one would expect the cohort to have been 75.3 percent satisfactory, practically the same result that occurred in the event. The Regional composition in fiscal 2007 actually favored the outcome—had the Regional composition remained unchanged, the overall fiscal 2007 outcome would have actually declined to 73.3 percent. The change in proportion of lending to conflict-affected and postconflict countries, or to

IDA versus IBRD lending, did not materially affect the outcomes. And the change in the sectoral composition and the share of projects utilizing special lending instruments was only marginally unfavorable (affecting the total by less than 2 percent).

Another possible explanation is that the drop in measured project performance is due to methodological changes in the way in which projects were evaluated in fiscal 2007. Some changes in methods were introduced by IEG and the Bank, together in fiscal 2007, to strengthen the robustness of project ratings and to cover new elements of project design. In the near term they may have introduced some element of discontinuity in the data series between fiscal 2007 and earlier years. It is estimated that the influence of methodology changes has been small—accounting for about 1 percentage point of the fall.

Besides these small changes in composition, what explains the weak performance of the fiscal 2007 cohort? It was driven by projects in health, financial and private sector development, and public sector governance, which performed very

Table A.1: Project Performance in FY07 Was Not Dependent on the Composition of the Cohort

Percentage of Satisfactory Projects		
Adjusting FY07 composition to reflect that of FY04–06 along the following dimensions:	**Would yield the following hypothetical outcomes:**	
Region	73.3	FY07 composition of projects was slightly favorable
Adjustment or investment	75.3	
Proportion of conflict- or postconflict-affected countries	75.7	
Actual FY07 Outcomes	**75.8 percent**	FY07 composition of projects had no effect
IDA, IBRD, GEF, or SPF	76.0	
Sector	76.7	FY07 composition of projects was slightly unfavorable
Lending instrument	77.5	

Source: World Bank database.

Note: Conflict- or postconflict-affected countries are those defined as such by the World Bank for any of the years fiscal 2003–06.

poorly relative to the Bank average, as well as projects in South Asia and Africa. In fiscal 2007, health, financial and private sector development, education and urban development showed major declines, when measured by the number of moderately satisfactory or better projects, as in South Asia, Africa, and Latin America, when compared with the prior 3-year period (see figure A.3). The portfolio of loans to conflict and postconflict countries also showed signs of worsening, with 76 percent moderately satisfactory or better in fiscal 2007, as compared with 82 percent in the previous three years. However, they still perform better than loans to nonconflict countries, of which only 69 percent were moderately satisfactory or better.

In fiscal 2007, there was a greater occurrence of five key factors influencing weak outcomes. First, poor or overly complex project design was a problem in more than half of underperforming loans, a finding also made by the World Bank's QAG (World Bank 2008a). For instance, two projects failed to recognize the importance of an appropriate legal and regulatory framework as a precondition to a privatization process. Several health projects failed to ensure a heightened focus on those interventions that would yield the greatest impact, leading for instance, to inadequate targeting of the poor, absence of a cost-effective package of health services, or inadequate funding for behavior change interventions to prevent HIV/AIDS transmission among high-risk groups.

Second, overambition was a weakness. While project objectives were almost always relevant, a majority was too far-reaching. Sometimes this was in terms of assessing political commitment and the feasibility of certain reforms. Other times it was in assessing government effectiveness and capacity, or in requiring coordination across several ministries or cumbersome financial management procedures that were not manageable by the parties involved. IEG's 2008 evaluation of public sector reform shows several examples where these factors led to unsatisfactory outcomes.

Third, delays in implementation caused difficulties, as circumstances changed and project design or implementation could not respond. About one-fifth of underperforming projects suffered from this problem.

Fourth, a majority of the unsatisfactory projects had a weak results framework, with poor or no baseline data, making it difficult to assess the outcomes of the project; and outcomes were often not well linked to inputs and outputs.

Finally, various gaps in the Bank's own performance contributed to a lack of success. For example, in spite of being flagged by the Bank's QAG as having poor quality at the outset, three projects were not reassessed or redesigned. The quality of the Bank's supervision was rated as moderately unsatisfactory or worse in two-thirds of all underperforming projects (and many such

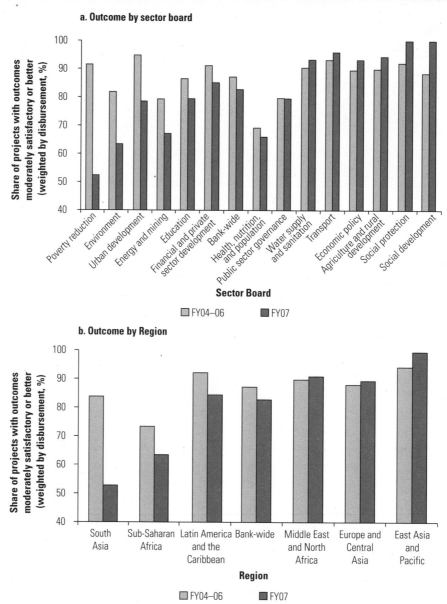

Figure A.3: Projects in Financial and Private Sector Development, Health, and Public Sector Governance Decline in FY07; South Asia and Africa Lag Behind

a. Outcome by sector board

FY04–06   FY07

Sector Board

b. Outcome by Region

FY04–06   FY07

Region

Source: World Bank database.

Note: Some changes in performance may be explained by a small sample size of projects that exited in fiscal 2007, including in the Environment (14 projects) and Poverty Reduction (4 projects) Sector Boards, and the South Asia Region (9 projects).

projects were not identified as problems in ongoing status reports). Bank overall performance—as distinct from borrower performance or the effects of uncontrollable events—was ranked moderately unsatisfactory or worse in two-thirds of these problem projects, compared with only about one-fifth of the full sample. All of this points

to a challenge in re-emphasizing a proactive quality control in management's attention to ongoing project performance

Sustainability and Institutional Development Impact

Under the new harmonized evaluation criteria

for project evaluations, approved in October 2005, projects would no longer be rated for their sustainability and institutional development impact (World Bank 2005b). Thus, only 122 of the 249 exit fiscal 2006 projects that were evaluated received a rating for their sustainability, and 132 for institutional development.

For this partial fiscal 2006 cohort, 83 percent of projects are rated likely or highly likely to be resilient to future risks, maintaining the fiscal 2005 rating for sustainability. Fifty-five percent of the partial fiscal 2006 cohort is rated substantial or high on institutional development impact, a small decline from fiscal 2005.[1] However, sustainability ratings represented a 10 percentage point increase, and institutional development impact ratings a 3 percentage point increase, for the fiscal 2006 (partial) cohort over the depressed fiscal 2003 cohort ratings (figure A.4).

Regional Performance

Figure A.5 presents the percentage of satisfactory project outcomes, weighted by disbursement, for the fiscal 2003–07 cohort, as compared with the fiscal 1998–2002 cohort. The East Asia and Pacific and Europe and Central Asia Regions

are the top performers for the fiscal 2003–07 cohort, exceeding the Bank average of 83 percent. The Latin America and Caribbean Region is the only one that declined in performance for the fiscal 2003–07 cohort. In spite of improving the most in performance for fiscal 2003–07, Africa continues to lag behind all other regions. Its performance declined in fiscal 2006 to 69 percent of outcomes moderately satisfactory or better, weighted by disbursement, and to 64 percent in fiscal 2007, an overall reduction of 10 percentage points from fiscal 2005.

Sectoral Performance

Compared with the fiscal 1998–2002 cohort, the outcome performance weighted by disbursement for the fiscal 2003–07 cohort improved in 8 of 12 sector boards.[2] Figure A.6 presents the sector boards' (and Bank-wide) outcome performance in order of their fiscal 2003–07 performance. The biggest improvements in outcome ratings were in water supply and sanitation, economic policy, energy and mining, and the social protection sector. The largest declines in performance were in health, nutrition, and population (which, along with economic policy and the environment, were significantly below

Figure A.4: Long-term Trends in Sustainability and Institutional Development

a.

b.

By number of projects   Weighted by value of project disbursements

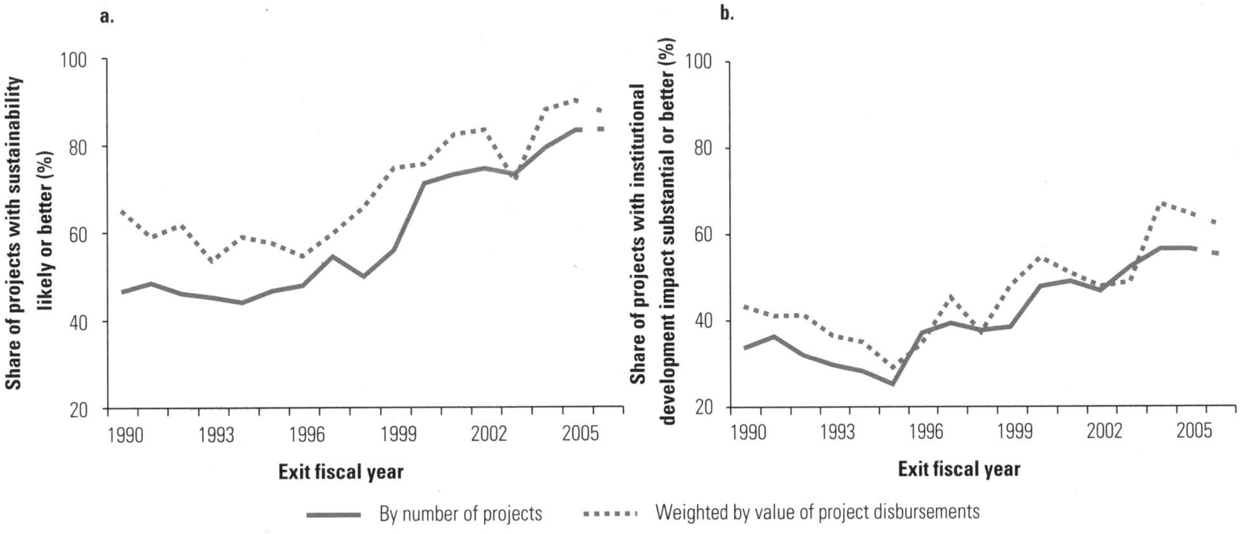

Source: World Bank database.

Note: Data for 2006 are partial (shown by dashed line).

Figure A.5: Africa Improves Relative to FY98–02, But Continues to Lag

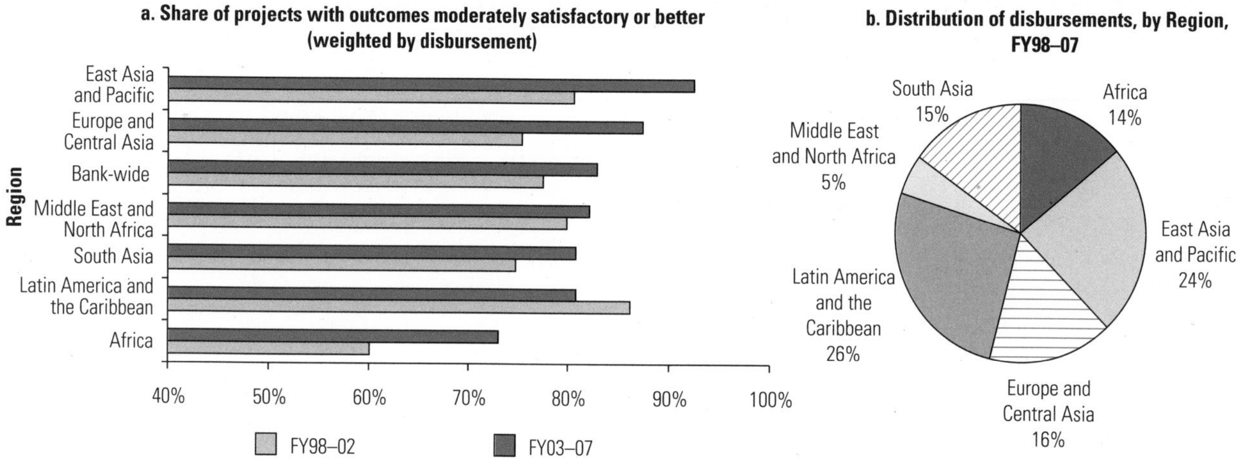

a. Share of projects with outcomes moderately satisfactory or better (weighted by disbursement)

b. Distribution of disbursements, by Region, FY98–07

FY98–02   FY03–07

Source: World Bank database.

the Bank-wide average for the fiscal 2003–07 period) and in public sector governance.

Lending Instrument Performance

The most recent data show a small dip in the share of development policy lending projects rated moderately satisfactory or better, both by number of projects and value of disbursements (see figure A.7) as measured on a three-year rolling average basis. Investment lending, too, has seen a decline in outcome performance.

New Lending Instruments

IEG has evaluated 241 operations employing the Bank's four new lending instruments—Adaptable Program Loans, Development Policy Loans, Learning and Innovation Loans, and Poverty Reduction Support Credits. More than 90 percent of these operations exited the Bank's portfolio during the fiscal 2003–07 period, amounting to $10.5 billion in disbursements, and 17 percent of all the projects that exited during that period. PRSCs have pulled up the performance of the group, exceeding the Bank average for the past five years of 77 percent and 82 percent, respectively, of moderately satisfactory or better projects and disbursements (figure A.8). Their outcome ratings have increased steadily since fiscal 2003 with 100 percent of

PRSCs being ranked satisfactory in fiscal 2006. Some of the project ratings are still provisional, however, with full ratings available for only 25 percent of PRSCs. IEG's ongoing evaluation of PRSCs will shed more light on the performance of this instrument. However, Learning and Innovation Loans are performing below the Bank average, and Adaptable Program Loan ratings have shown a decline in the two years since fiscal 2005 in performance, but an increase as a proportion of the portfolio in fiscal 2007. Twenty-one Development Policy Loans, the newest Bank instrument, have been rated so far, and have performed just above the Bank average, weighted by disbursement, over fiscal 2003–07.

Bank-Managed Special Programs

IEG has evaluated 87 operations financed under four Bank-managed special programs that have exited the Bank's portfolio since fiscal 2003 (table A.2). Seventy-seven percent of the special operations had satisfactory outcomes, a decline of 8 percent as compared with operations exiting between fiscal 1998 and fiscal 2002. This decline in performance is mainly due to the lower satisfactory outcomes of Special Financing Grants or multidonor-sponsored trust funds that have assisted five conflict-affected or postconflict countries in the past decade.[3] The resources

Figure A.6: Trends in Sectoral Performance

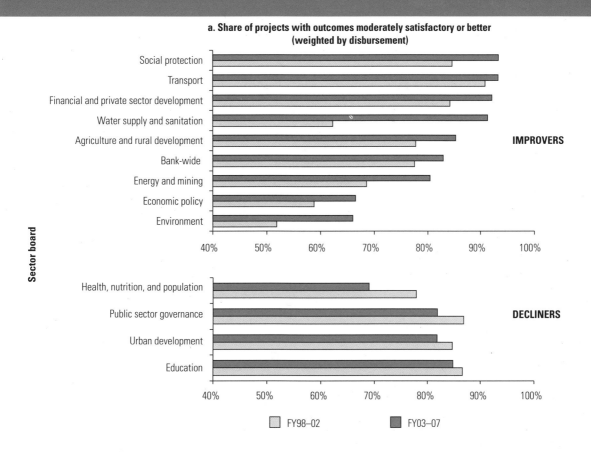

a. Share of projects with outcomes moderately satisfactory or better (weighted by disbursement)

IMPROVERS

DECLINERS

FY98–02   FY03–07

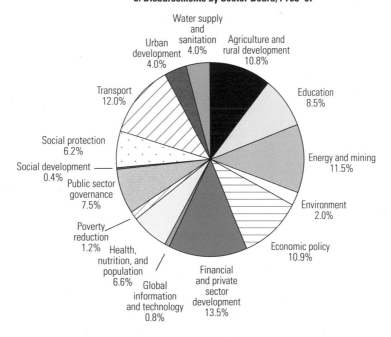

b. Disbursements by Sector Board, FY98–07

Water supply and sanitation 4.0%

Urban development 4.0%

Agriculture and rural development 10.8%

Transport 12.0%

Education 8.5%

Social protection 6.2%

Energy and mining 11.5%

Social development 0.4%

Public sector governance 7.5%

Environment 2.0%

Poverty reduction 1.2%

Economic policy 10.9%

Health, nutrition, and population 6.6%

Global information and technology 0.8%

Financial and private sector development 13.5%

Source: World Bank database.

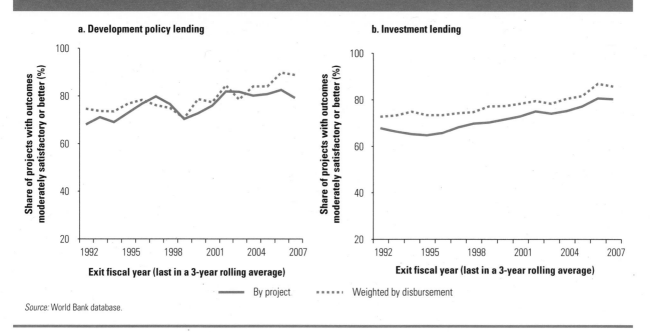

Figure A.7: Long-Term Trends in Development Policy Lending and Investment Lending

a. Development policy lending

b. Investment lending

Exit fiscal year (last in a 3-year rolling average)

——— By project   ∙∙∙∙∙∙ Weighted by disbursement

Source: World Bank database.

devoted to Special Financing Grants exiting between fiscal 2003 and fiscal 2007 were $493 million, or 0.5 percent of the Bank's overall project portfolio during this period.[4]

Figure A.8: Outcome Performance of New Lending Instruments

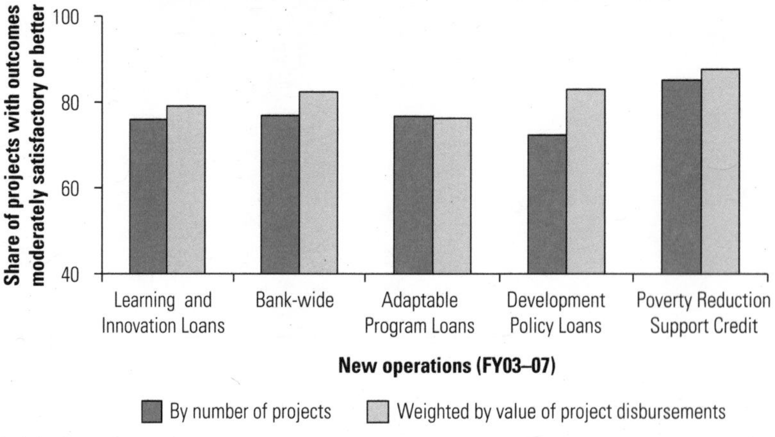

New operations (FY03–07)

■ By number of projects   □ Weighted by value of project disbursements

Source: World Bank database.

Table A.2: Bank-Managed Special Programs Are Performing on Par with Bank Average

Special program type	Exit FY98–02			Exit FY03–07		
	Number of evaluated projects	Disbursements (% of World Bank portfolio)	Outcome: % satisfactory[a]	Number of evaluated projects	Disbursements (% of World Bank portfolio)	Outcome: % satisfactory[a]
Global Environment Facility	39	0.1	79.5	39	0.46	84.6
Montreal Protocol Fund	4	0.0	100.0	5	0.05	100.0
Rainforest Initiative	1	0.0	100.0	2	0.00	100.0
Special Financing Grants	17	0.2	94.1	41	0.54	65.9
All Special Programs	61	0.3	85.2	87	1.0	77.0

Source: World Bank database.

a. Projects whose outcomes are rated moderately satisfactory, satisfactory, or highly satisfactory are here referred to as "satisfactory."

Table A.3: Outcome, Sustainability, and Institutional Development (ID) Impact by Various Dimensions, by Project, FY98–07

	Exit FY98–02				
	Number of projects	Share (%)	Outcome: % satisfactory[a]	Sustainability: % likely or better	ID impact: % substantial or better
Sector Board					
Agriculture and Rural Development	229	16	66.4	53.7	37.8
Economic Policy	74	5	56.8	65.2	29.7
Education	133	10	81.2	66.9	40.6
Energy and Mining	153	11	68.0	59.4	43.3
Environment	72	5	71.8	73.9	50.7
Financial and Private Sector Development	159	11	64.9	66.4	38.8
Gender and Development		0	na	na	na
Global Information/Communications Technology	16	1	100.0	100.0	68.8
Health, Nutrition, and Population	108	8	65.7	61.0	36.9
Poverty Reduction		0	na	na	na
Public Sector Governance	98	7	84.4	79.8	54.2
Social Development	1	0	100.0	100.0	100.0
Social Protection	84	6	83.1	58.3	45.8
Transport	137	10	88.0	78.4	64.7
Urban Development	67	5	71.2	50.0	36.4
Water Supply and Sanitation	67	5	65.2	46.9	33.3
Overall Result	*1,398*	*100*	*72.5*	*63.8*	*43.4*
Lending Instrument Type					
Dev Pol Lending	177	13	75.1	73.8	43.2
Investment	1220	87	72.1	62.3	43.4
Not Assigned	1	0	100.0	100.0	0.0
Overall Result	*1,398*	*100*	*72.5*	*63.8*	*43.4*
Network					
Financial and Private Sector Development	172	12	66.5	64.7	38.8
Human Development	325	23	76.6	62.8	40.8
Poverty Reduction & Economic Management	172	12	72.4	73.4	43.5
Sustainable Development	729	52	72.1	61.8	45.5
Overall Result	*1,398*	*100*	*72.5*	*63.8*	*43.4*
Region					
Africa	385	28	59.5	47.1	32.4
East Asia and Pacific	206	15	76.2	64.4	45.5
Europe and Central Asia	274	20	82.8	80.2	52.4
Latin America and Caribbean	277	20	76.4	69.4	50.8
Middle East and North Africa	105	8	73.8	64.9	39.8
Not Assigned	0	0	na	na	na
South Asia	151	11	74.2	64.8	41.1
Overall Result	*1,398*	*100*	*72.5*	*63.8*	*43.4*
Agreement Type					
Not Assigned	1	0	100.0	100.0	100.0
Global Environmental Facility	39	3	79.5	63.2	51.3
IBRD	671	48	75.9	71.6	48.7
IDA	665	48	67.9	55.5	37.4
Montreal Protocol Fund	4	0	100.0	100.0	75.0
Rainforest Initiative	1	0	100.0	100.0	0.0
Special Financing Grants	17	1	94.1	71.4	41.2
Overall Result	*1,398*	*100*	*72.5*	*63.8*	*43.4*

Source: World Bank database.

na = not applicable.

a. Projects whose outcomes are rated moderately satisfactory, satisfactory, or highly satisfactory are here referred to as "satisfactory."

	Exit FY03–07					Exit FY98–07			
Number of projects	Share (%)	Outcome: % satisfactory[a]	Sustainability: % likely or better	ID impact: % substantial or better	Number of projects	Share (%)	Outcome: % satisfactory[a]	Sustainability: % likely or better	ID impact: % substantial or better
188	14	83.1	78.0	60.1	417	15	73.9	62.5	46.5
76	6	81.1	80.0	41.0	150	5	68.9	71.4	34.8
136	10	81.3	85.4	59.8	269	10	81.3	74.6	48.7
83	6	77.5	80.0	67.9	236	9	71.3	64.8	49.8
84	6	75.3	73.1	52.5	156	6	73.7	73.6	51.5
124	9	72.1	80.7	56.1	283	10	68.1	71.9	45.6
1	0	100.0	100.0	100.0	1	0	100.0	100.0	100.0
11	1	100.0	100.0	50.0	27	1	100.0	100.0	62.5
109	8	61.5	72.6	59.2	217	8	63.6	65.9	46.4
21	2	81.0	90.9	53.8	21	1	81.0	90.9	53.8
124	9	64.5	74.4	41.9	222	8	73.3	77.1	48.1
23	2	71.4	66.7	42.9	24	1	72.7	69.2	46.7
96	7	83.0	74.5	50.0	180	7	83.1	65.0	47.7
119	9	92.4	86.5	62.7	256	9	90.0	81.4	63.9
78	6	79.2	77.0	44.8	145	5	75.5	63.2	40.6
71	5	84.3	78.8	59.6	138	5	75.0	61.2	45.5
1,344	*100*	*78.1*	*78.9*	*54.8*	*2,742*	*100*	*75.2*	*69.9*	*48.1*
202	15	79.8	88.1	52.6	379	14	77.6	80.3	47.6
1,140	85	77.7	77.1	55.1	2,360	86	74.8	68.2	48.2
2	0	100.0	100.0	100.0	3	0	100.0	100.0	50.0
1,344	*100*	*78.1*	*78.9*	*54.8*	*2,742*	*100*	*75.2*	*69.9*	*48.1*
124	9	72.1	80.7	56.1	296	11	68.9	70.5	45.2
341	25	75.4	78.4	56.8	666	24	76.0	69.4	47.7
222	17	71.9	77.7	42.9	394	14	72.1	75.5	43.2
657	49	82.7	79.1	57.6	1,386	51	77.1	68.5	50.4
1,344	*100*	*78.1*	*78.9*	*54.8*	*2,742*	*100*	*75.2*	*69.9*	*48.1*
316	24	67.1	66.3	47.7	701	26	62.9	54.2	38.3
202	15	83.5	80.9	64.4	408	15	79.9	71.2	53.6
282	21	83.2	89.6	62.9	556	20	83.0	84.4	57.0
318	24	82.6	81.3	56.7	595	22	79.7	74.6	53.4
111	8	73.6	70.9	33.7	216	8	73.7	67.6	37.0
1	0	100.0	na	na	1	0	100.0	na	na
114	8.5	78.1	83.8	54.8	265	9.7	75.8	71.3	46.0
1,344	*100*	*78.1*	*78.9*	*54.8*	*2,742*	*100*	*75.2*	*69.9*	*48.1*
0	0	na	na	na	1	0	100.0	100.0	100.0
39	3	84.6	76.2	53.8	78	3	82.1	67.8	52.3
603	45	82.3	83.9	57.6	1,274	46	78.9	76.6	52.4
654	49	74.4	75.7	53.2	1,319	48	71.1	63.6	44.0
5	0	100.0	100.0	50.0	9	0	100.0	100.0	66.7
2	0	100.0	100.0	100.0	3	0	100.0	100.0	50.0
41	3.1	65.9	48.2	37.5	58	2.12	74.1	56.1	38.8
1,344	*100*	*78.1*	*78.9*	*54.8*	*2,742*	*100*	*75.2*	*69.9*	*48.1*

Table A.4: Outcome, Sustainability, and Institutional Development (ID) Impact by Various Dimensions, by Disbursement, FY98–07

	Exit FY98–02				
	Disburse-ments ($m)	Share (%)	Outcome: % satisfactory[a]	Sustainability: % likely or better	ID impact: % substantial or better
Sector Board					
Agriculture and Rural Development	11,669	11	77.8	67.3	45.4
Economic Policy	11,497	11	51.9	77.5	37.7
Education	8,125	8	86.6	76.4	44.7
Energy and Mining	15,234	14	68.6	62.3	44.0
Environment	1,517	1	58.8	84.9	37.4
Financial and Private Sector Development	18,019	17	84.1	85.9	51.3
Gender and Development	0	0	na	na	na
Global Information/Communications Technology	1,297	1	100.0	100.0	61.5
Health, Nutrition, and Population	5,622	5	77.9	74.5	45.8
Poverty Reduction	0	0	na	na	na
Public Sector Governance	7,638	7	86.8	91.1	52.0
Social Development	5	0	100.0	100.0	100.0
Social Protection	6,289	6	84.5	77.1	40.9
Transport	11,908	11	90.8	85.1	66.0
Urban Development	3,868	4	84.6	56.7	40.8
Water Supply and Sanitation	4,342	4	62.3	40.4	26.1
Overall Result	*107,031*	*100*	*77.5*	*74.9*	*46.8*
Lending Instrument Type					
Dev Pol Lending	38,247	36	77.6	84.8	46.0
Investment	68,783	64	77.5	69.7	47.3
Not Assigned	0	0	na	na	na
Overall Result	*107,031*	*100*	*77.5*	*74.9*	*46.8*
Network					
Financial and Private Sector Development	19,658	18	84.2	82.3	48.9
Human Development	20,036	19	83.5	76.1	43.8
Poverty Reduction & Economic Management	19,135	18	65.8	83.0	43.4
Sustainable Development	48,202	45	77.0	68.7	48.8
Overall Result	*107,031*	*100*	*77.5*	*74.9*	*46.8*
Region					
Africa	13,143	12	60.0	48.5	28.7
East Asia and Pacific	28,502	27	80.6	81.4	50.3
Europe and Central Asia	19,187	18	75.3	82.6	51.4
Latin America and Caribbean	25,040	23	86.2	80.1	54.5
Middle East and North Africa	5,544	5	79.9	67.3	49.4
Not Assigned	0	0	na	na	na
South Asia	15,616	15	74.7	70.8	37.5
Overall Result	*107,031*	*100*	*77.5*	*74.9*	*46.8*
Agreement Type					
Not Assigned	32	0	100.0	100.0	100.0
Global Environment Facility	138	0	80.0	69.6	55.6
IBRD	79,302	74	78.5	78.5	50.0
IDA	27,332	26	74.6	64.9	38.1
Montreal Protocol Fund	9	0	100.0	100.0	81.4
Rainforest Initiative	0	0	na	na	na
Special Financing Grants	219	0	96.8	69.2	33.4
Overall Result	*107,031*	*100*	*77.5*	*74.9*	*46.8*

Source: World Bank database.

na = not applicable.

a. Projects whose outcomes are rated moderately satisfactory, satisfactory, or highly satisfactory are here referred to as "satisfactory."

	Exit FY03–07					Exit FY98–07			
Disburse-ments ($m)	Share (%)	Outcome: % satisfactory[a]	Sustainability: % likely or better	ID impact: % substantial or better	Disburse-ments ($m)	Share (%)	Outcome: % satisfactory[a]	Sustainability: % likely or better	ID impact: % substantial or better
9,800	11	85.2	82.2	70.3	21,469	11	81.2	73.0	55.1
10,081	11	65.9	55.6	27.3	21,578	11	58.4	67.6	33.0
8,798	10	84.7	95.5	70.2	16,922	9	85.6	85.0	56.3
7,635	8	80.4	76.3	74.4	22,869	12	72.5	65.7	51.4
2,393	3	66.4	76.9	40.4	3,911	2	63.0	80.3	39.1
8,847	10	92.1	95.6	81.0	26,866	14	86.8	89.0	61.4
3	0	100.0	100.0	100.0	3	0	100.0	100.0	100.0
214	0	100.0	100.0	33.2	1,511	1	100.0	100.0	58.0
7,426	8	69.0	78.2	61.1	13,048	7	72.8	76.1	52.6
2,287	3	84.8	92.5	28.9	2,287	1	84.8	92.5	28.9
7,337	8	81.8	88.2	51.8	14,975	8	84.3	89.8	51.9
847	1	65.4	94.2	44.2	852	0	65.6	94.2	44.6
6,025	7	93.3	85.2	72.2	12,313	6	88.8	79.5	51.9
11,906	13	93.3	90.4	60.9	23,814	12	92.0	87.3	63.9
4,156	5	81.7	80.6	53.0	8,024	4	83.1	68.6	46.9
3,598	4	91.3	78.8	66.1	7,941	4	75.4	55.8	42.3
91,353	*100*	*82.8*	*82.5*	*59.3*	*198,383*	*100*	*80.0*	*77.9*	*51.8*
30,125	33	82.2	81.9	53.1	68,372	34	79.6	83.7	48.9
61,228	67	83.1	82.9	62.7	130,011	66	80.1	74.9	53.4
0	0	na	na	na	0	0	na	na	na
91,353	*100*	*82.8*	*82.5*	*59.3*	*198,383*	*100*	*80.0*	*77.9*	*51.8*
8,847	10	92.1	95.6	81.0	28,505	14	86.7	86.2	59.1
22,248	24	81.8	87.8	67.9	42,284	21	82.6	80.9	54.0
19,708	22	74.0	70.7	35.7	38,843	20	70.0	77.2	39.8
40,549	44	85.6	82.8	62.8	88,751	45	80.9	74.1	54.2
91,353	*100*	*82.8*	*82.5*	*59.3*	*198,383*	*100*	*80.0*	*77.9*	*51.8*
14,572	16	73.0	74.8	52.0	27,714	14	66.9	60.1	39.2
18,261	20	92.4	90.2	74.7	46,763	24	85.2	84.2	59.0
12,053	13	87.4	92.9	70.7	31,240	16	80.0	86.4	58.2
28,920	32	80.8	73.7	56.4	53,960	27	83.3	77.3	55.4
4,032	4	82.1	82.3	31.2	9,575	5	80.8	72.5	43.1
0	0	na	na	na	0	0	na	na	na
13,491	15	80.8	87.8	48.5	29,107	15	77.5	77.5	41.8
91,353	*100*	*82.8*	*82.5*	*59.3*	*198,383*	*100*	*80.0*	*77.9*	*51.8*
0	0	na	na	na	32	0	100.0	100.0	100.0
422	0	90.9	91.8	52.3	560	0	88.2	84.1	53.3
58,907	64	84.7	82.9	62.4	138,209	70	81.1	80.1	54.6
31,487	34	79.4	82.1	53.8	58,820	30	77.1	72.5	45.3
43	0	100.0	100.0	4.0	52	0	100.0	100.0	21.2
0	0	na	na	na	0	0	na	na	na
493	1	66.9	44.3	25.8	712	0	76.1	52.8	28.5
91,353	*100*	*82.8*	*82.5*	*59.3*	*198,383*	*100*	*80.0*	*77.9*	*51.8*

APPENDIX B: MONITORING AND EVALUATION OVERVIEW

The Bank has in place the policies and procedures to monitor, self-evaluate, and conduct independent evaluation of its operations. The Regions conduct the monitoring and self-evaluating of their lending, analytical, and advisory activities, and country assistance programs under guidelines issued by the Operations Policy and Country Services Vice-Presidency. Monitoring and self-evaluation of operations Bank-wide is carried out by the Quality Assurance Group, Operations Policy and Country Services, and other units. The Bank is also strengthening its monitoring and self-evaluation activities financed through trust funds and its involvement in global programs and partnerships.

Independent evaluation is carried out by IEG. The Director-General of Evaluation reports directly to the Executive Board, which approves the Director-General's mandate and IEG's terms of reference. IEG validates the Bank's self-evaluations, verifies their results, and assesses the relevance, efficacy, and efficiency of Bank operational activities and processes.

The Bank formally revised some of its policies to better monitor and evaluate the results of Bank operations. The Bank issued a new OP/BP 8.60, *Development Policy Lending*, in 2004, requiring outcomes and measurable indicators for M&E in policy loans/credits as well as investment projects. BP 2.11, *Country Assistance Strategies*, was updated in 2005, mainstreaming the results-based country assistance strategy approach. In 2007, the Bank revised OP 13.60, which had focused on dissemination and utilization of IEG findings, making it a policy on M&E. The new OP 13.60, *Monitoring and Evaluation*, includes a section on Bank monitoring and self-evaluation and another on independent evaluation, outlining IEG's role. OP/BP 14.40, *Trust Funds*, also provides guidance on monitoring and evaluation for activities falling under that rubric, and has been updated to introduce enhancements, including greater coverage of periodic independent evaluation.

Table B.1: Summary of Bank Monitoring and Evaluation

Type of intervention or instrument	MONITORING	
	Defining outcomes and monitoring indicators	Tracking and reporting on implementation progress
Loans and credits	Results frameworks in Project Appraisal Documents (for investment loan/credits) and Program Documents (for development policy loans/credits)	Implementation Status Report
Analytical and advisory activities	Concept paper specifies development objectives and tracking indicators	Activity update summary
Country programs	Results framework in Country Assistance Strategy	CAS Progress Report
Trust-funded activities	Initiating Brief for Trust Fund includes program objectives and accompanying performance indicators	Grant reporting and monitoring system for child trust fund/grant

Source: IEG.

	EVALUATION	
	Independent evaluation by IEG	
Self-evaluation	**Individual activity**	**Aggregate level**
• Ex post: Implementation Completion and Results Reports	ICR reviews (all); Project Performance Assessment Report (selected)	ARDE
• Ex ante: QAG Quality-at-Entry Assessments.		
• Bank-wide: QAG Annual Report on Portfolio Performance		
• Ex post: Activity completion summary	Reviewed as part of sector/thematic and country assistance evaluations	
• Country: QAG analytic and advisory activity assessments		
• Bank-wide: QAG Annual Report on Portfolio Performance		
• Ex post: CASCR	• CASCR reviews;	ARDE, sector/thematic evaluations
• Bank-wide: CAS retrospectives.	• Country Assistance Evaluations	
• Less than $1 million: grant report and monitoring completion report		
• More than $1 million: Implementation Completion and Results Report		

Overview

IEG contributes to the Bank's effectiveness by supporting the Board's oversight function and promoting learning within the Bank and the development community. One tool to gather feedback on IEG's work is a client survey, albeit any such survey has limitations, with respect to sample size and scale of response. The most recent survey found that among respondents, both inside and outside the Bank, there was some increase in awareness of IEG's products. Compared with earlier years, an increasing proportion of respondents reported general satisfaction with the quality and timeliness of IEG products. But they gave IEG lower marks for depth of analysis and incorporation of all available information. The use of evaluations for oversight among World Bank Executive Directors who responded to the survey remains high. Use of evaluation findings in the design of new operations by respondents who are operational staff was higher in 2007 than a year earlier, but remains low.

The lower ratings for operational use and satisfaction with depth of analysis point to the challenge of finding the right breadth and length for IEG products. IEG's work program for fiscal 2009–11, discussed with CODE in May 2008, assembles a good mix of activities, including increased emphasis on newer products such as CASCR reviews, clustered Project Performance Assessment Reports, and quicker turnaround reports on selected major issues of topical interest.

Beyond client feedback, the Management Action Record (MAR) allows IEG to track its recommenda-

tions from sector, thematic, and corporate evaluations. Bank management is accountable to the Board for follow-up. The MAR tracks the level of adoption and the status of individual recommendations. It presents management's ratings on these two indicators and IEG's assessment of the same.

The 2008 MAR shows a continuing high level of agreement by the Bank with IEG's recommendations. Some 96 percent of IEG proposals made in the last three years' evaluations have been accepted by the Bank. In terms of the Bank then adopting those recommendations and putting them into practice, some 95 percent have been adopted with medium, substantial, or high ratings, a level slightly above the previous year. However, the share of recommendations adopted with substantial or high ratings was 42 percent, which is below the level of previous years.

Going forward, the challenge is for IEG to continue producing high-quality evaluations with sensible and practical recommendations, retain the high level of agreement on those recommendations, and for the Bank to lift its intensity of adoption and implementation.

Improving IEG's Effectiveness

This appendix provides an overview of IEG's role in improving the Bank's development effectiveness. It includes a results framework that links IEG's mandate and objectives to its operations. Within this framework, the appendix updates IEG's efforts to increase its evaluation focus on results. The appendix includes findings from the annual client survey, an update on the communications and outreach strategy, and the status of the MAR.

IEG's Results Framework

IEG has three functions in improving development effectiveness. First, it provides accountability by independently reporting on the results achieved by Bank operations. Second, it distills the Bank's operational experience into knowledge of what works and why, and makes that knowledge widely available to Bank personnel and the global development community. Third, it supports client governments with its technical knowledge on M&E through its evaluation capacity development activities.

IEG has a mandate to assess "whether the World Bank Group's programs and activities are producing the expected results, including global, regional, and other programs in which the World Bank Group is a participant."[1] By reporting the results of its evaluations to the Board of Directors and communicating the findings and lessons from its work to Bank management, operational staff, and the development community, IEG expects to increase the Bank's effectiveness and influence Bank and client country decisions on policies, programs, and procedures. While fully independent,[2] IEG is placed within the Bank to maximize its operational effectiveness and to provide operational staff and strategic decision makers with knowledge that helps them work more effectively.

IEG's results chain is summarized in figure C.1, and related to measures of performance that have been collected for this report. IEG's outputs are the findings, lessons, and recommendations from its evaluations, and evaluation capacity support in client countries. Dissemination efforts are the intermediate step between outputs and outcomes. For IEG's accountability function, the intermediate outcomes of these outputs are the use of evaluations by the Board to fulfill its oversight function, and the incorporation of IEG recommendations in Bank internal policies and procedures. For IEG's function as a knowledge provider, the intermediate outcome of IEG's outputs is the influence and use of these outputs to improve the Bank's policy advice and program and project design. It also includes use of these outputs by external partners to improve their development work.

The final outcome for IEG outputs is the use of IEG knowledge about what works and why, leading to improved effectiveness of Bank operations, and development assistance in general, in reducing poverty. For example, IEG's evaluation of regional programs has contributed significantly to the recognition of the importance of regional approaches for the delivery of global public goods (GPGs) by the Bank.[3] Outside the Bank, the Bill and Melinda Gates Foundation used IEG's recent evaluation of World Bank Assistance to Agriculture in Sub-Saharan Africa (2007d) as one of the main sources for the development of its agriculture strategy. The Bank's operational staff, management, Board, and external clients use IEG's outputs to strengthen actions taken in client countries. Measures that attribute achievement of the final outcome to IEG, however, are difficult to construct.

Underscoring the importance of the above results framework, the 2006 AROE recommended that "To further strengthen IEG's contribution to the workings of the results agenda in the World Bank Group, IEG should continue to follow its own results framework and monitor it through the AROE. Its focus on the usefulness of evaluation findings for its core audiences should be enhanced: for the **Board** through oversight, for **management** through the incorporation of recommendations into Bank policies and strategies, for **Bank staff** through the use of evaluation findings for policy advice to country partners and in project design, for **external partners** through the use of evaluation findings to improve their programs and policies, and for the **countries** more broadly. In playing this role, IEG should specifically:

- Improve the timeliness of its evaluations,
- Strengthen the operational relevance of the findings, and
- Increase access to and exchange of the lessons."

This appendix describes the key links in IEG's results chain, giving special attention to the recommendations from last year, and highlights recent developments in the results of IEG's

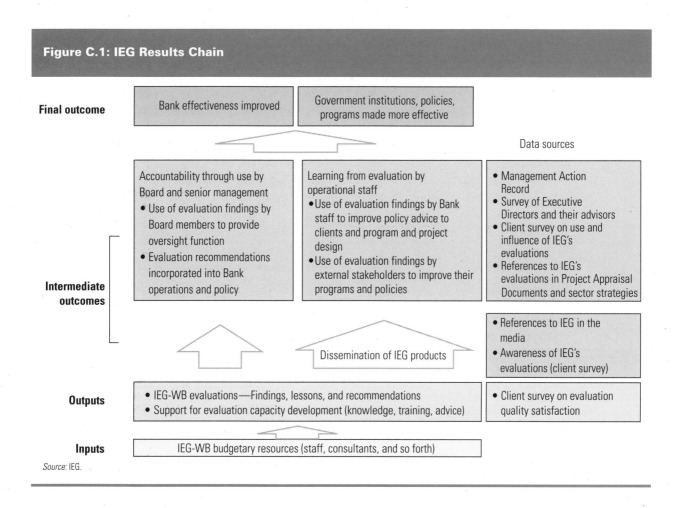

Figure C.1: IEG Results Chain

Source: IEG.

approach. First, it looks at the activities IEG has undertaken to improve its output and the achievement of outcomes; and second, it analyzes the change in indicators that measure the quality of outputs and achievement of IEG's outcomes.

IEG's Outputs: Increasing Relevance and the Focus on Learning

At the product level, IEG has continued its line of quickly produced papers that address immediate needs for evaluative findings and lessons of experience, in the form of notes, presentations, or briefing papers. IEG's short papers, in 2007, on governance received especially positive feedback. IEG's work plan for fiscal 2009–11 continues the shift to fewer and more influential evaluations, including some shorter, topical products, and an increasing number of evaluations conducted jointly across IEG (World Bank, International Finance Corporation, and Multilateral Investment Guarantee Association).

At the level of country evaluation, the adoption of CASCR reviews[4] represents a major shift in the Bank's evaluation system, because it ensures systematic evaluation coverage of CAS results. In CASCR reviews, IEG reviews the relevance of the CAS to the country's development priorities, implementation of the country program, achievement of CAS objectives, and the quality of the CASCR itself. IEG then gives a rating for CAS implementation and Bank performance.[5] As of March 2008, IEG has reviewed 59 CASCRs, 17 of which were completed in fiscal 2007. Going forward, IEG is planning to review up to 30 CASCRs each year. Besides its rating function, the CASCR review is intended as a learning tool that distills lessons learned from implementation of the preceding CAS for incorporation into the design and implementation of the following CAS. To make its country reviews more useful and relevant, IEG is also planning an enhanced CASCR review, which would combine the timely delivery of IEG's results, when the new CAS is discussed at the Board, with the insights of a country mission which would allow a much more thorough assessment of CAS achievements and challenges by IEG.

It has to be noted, however, that the existing process limits the effectiveness of the CASCR review as a learning tool. IEG receives the final CASCR for validation when the preparation of the new CAS is nearly complete. Therefore, it may be too late for the country team to incorporate much, if any, of IEG's findings directly into the CAS document. But lessons learned on the implementation of the CAS should be considered by the country team as it moves to implement the new CAS. This issue has not been addressed so far. In the case of enhanced CASCR reviews, it would be even more important because these would need more preparation time.

To create incentives within the Bank for good performance in design, implementation, M&E, and development effectiveness, IEG has been giving annual Good Practice Awards to operations that exemplify strong performance in these areas.[6] In addition to providing incentives for high performance, the awards heighten the profile of operations that offer examples of good practices. To foster the exchange of lessons between operational staff and to highlight the importance of mutual learning, IEG added a learning event to the 2007 and 2008 awards ceremonies (see box C.1).

Deepening Strategic Partnerships

IEG's success in achieving greater focus on results and learning requires strategic partnerships. For example, to capitalize on the impact evaluation expertise available in other groups in the Bank, IEG has been collaborating with the thematic group for poverty analysis, monitoring, impact evaluation, and the Development Economics Department. Together, the three groups organized a two-day event in January 2008, *Making Smart Policy: Using Impact Evaluation for Policy Making.*

Evaluation capacity development. IEG is strengthening its support of results-oriented monitoring and evaluation systems and capacities in client countries. As a result of its 2004 self-evaluation of evaluation capacity development, IEG refocused its high-intensity support on a few targeted, demonstration countries while maintaining low-intensity support to a much broader range of countries. In recent years, these efforts were particularly evident for Colombia, Mexico, and China, and this support will now be extended to other regions. Also, in June 2008, IEG hosted the annual International Program in Development Evaluation Training (IPDET), in collaboration with Carleton University, for the eighth time. This

---

Box C.1: IEG Good Practice Awards: Secrets of Successful Operations— An IEG Learning Event

Since 2004, the World Bank's Independent Evaluation Group (IEG) has selected a small number of winners, from among operations evaluated in the previous fiscal year, for its Annual Good Practice Awards. The main objective is to highlight exemplary design, implementation, and self-evaluation in Bank projects and country programs, and to create incentives among Bank staff for greater learning from evaluation, to enhance development effectiveness.

To facilitate replication of these good practices in other operations, in 2007 and 2008, IEG invited Good Practice Award winners to share their experiences and lessons learned with other Bank staff in a learning event, Secrets of Successful Operations. In these engaging discussions, Bank experts—including award winners from the Europe and Central Asia and the Latin America and Caribbean Regions, who led the way in using evaluation effectively—helped identify the challenges they faced in their work and what they did to address them. The experts offered lessons for future operations and participants were encouraged to identify specific lessons to apply to their own work.

four-week course draws broad interest from evaluation professionals and policy makers worldwide. In addition, IEG has a formal partnership with the Chinese government to help develop a regional center for development evaluation training in Shanghai, and a regional version of the development evaluation training is offered there on a twice-yearly basis. Since its inception in 2001, more than two thousand practitioners have participated in the International Program in Development Evaluation Training. Evaluation capacity development products on M&E methodology, impact evaluation, and influential evaluations consistently draw strong interest among practitioners.

Harmonizing development evaluation. As the largest and oldest of the evaluation units in the multilateral development banks, IEG has taken a leadership role in harmonization efforts among the international evaluation community. IEG has actively promoted harmonization of development evaluation methods through the multilateral development banks' Evaluation Cooperation Group, the Development Assistance Committee Evaluation Network, and the United Nations Evaluation Group. The Evaluation Cooperation Group has developed good practice standards for evaluation of both public and private sector development work. Member institutions have been benchmarked against these standards. Beyond that, IEG led the work on a joint Evaluation Cooperation Group paper synthesizing findings and lessons on the linkages between infrastructure and environment operations. IEG took the lead in creating the Network of Networks on Impact Evaluation, with members such as the Development Assistance Committee Evaluation Network, the Evaluation Cooperation Group, and the United Nations Evaluation Group, as well as developing countries and NGOs. IEG is providing the secretariat for this group, which is developing good practice standards for development impact evaluation and promoting impact evaluations of development work. IEG also led the Development Assistance Committee Evaluation Network's work on developing good practice standards and guidelines for evaluating global and regional programs.

Quality and Relevance of IEG Outputs: Results of the 2007 Client Survey

IEG measures the quality and relevance of its outputs as part of its annual internal and external client surveys. The 2007 surveys asked target audiences for their views of IEG products prepared in 2006 and 2007, including 5 sector and thematic studies, 5 corporate reports, 6 CAEs, about 40 Project Performance Assessment Reports, and an evaluation capacity development report. IEG surveyed a targeted sample of 4,218 internal clients, consisting of Bank staff and Executive Directors and their advisors. The response rate was 24 percent, as compared with 22 percent last year.[7] The survey of external clients on published evaluations approached a sample of 6,238 individuals and achieved a response rate of 19 percent. Given these response rates, it has to be noted that the survey results are indicative for respondents, but cannot be generalized to the surveyed population.

Readership and awareness. Sixty-one percent of Bank staff who responded to the most recent annual client survey (2007) were aware of the evaluation for which they were surveyed. This is above the 56 percent in 2006 and continues the trend of increasing awareness of IEG products among Bank staff respondents, only 39 percent of whom indicated awareness in 2004. Among respondents to the external survey, 75 percent were aware of the evaluation for which they were surveyed, compared with 76 percent in 2006.

The quality of IEG evaluations. As shown in figure C.2, Bank staff were asked to rate their satisfaction with IEG's evaluation for 10 attributes of quality on a six-point scale. Bank staff respondents were more satisfied with the quality of IEG products in 2007 than in 2006, across all attributes of quality. Bank staff respondents continue to report highest satisfaction with the relevance of IEG's evaluations to their work, with 80 percent of respondents rating it 4 or higher, the highest rating in the past four years. Bank staff respondents continue to be least satisfied with the incorporation of all available information and the depth of analysis, with 63 percent and 66 percent of respondents expressing their satisfaction, respectively.

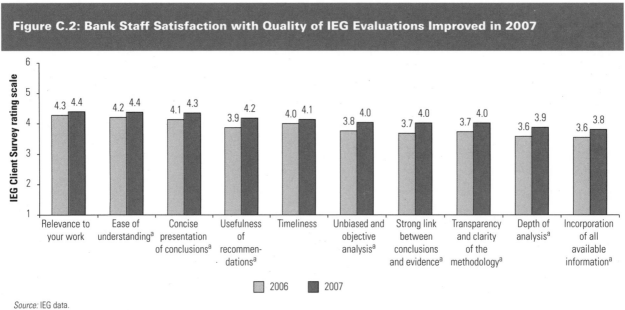

Figure C.2: Bank Staff Satisfaction with Quality of IEG Evaluations Improved in 2007

Source: IEG data.

Note: Bars show the means on a six-point scale, where 1 = highly unsatisfied, and 6 = highly satisfied. The sample size for 2006 is 292, for 2007 is 417.

a. Difference is significant at 90 percent confidence level.

Due to changes in the survey methodology, a longer time series is only possible for a few quality attributes. Figure C.3 shows that IEG continuously improved the timeliness and relevance of its products to operational staff. Regarding views on the depth of analysis in IEG evaluations, the decline in ratings stopped in 2007, but there is room for improvement.

Executive Directors and their advisors who responded to the survey are very satisfied with the quality of IEG products. As figure C.4 shows,

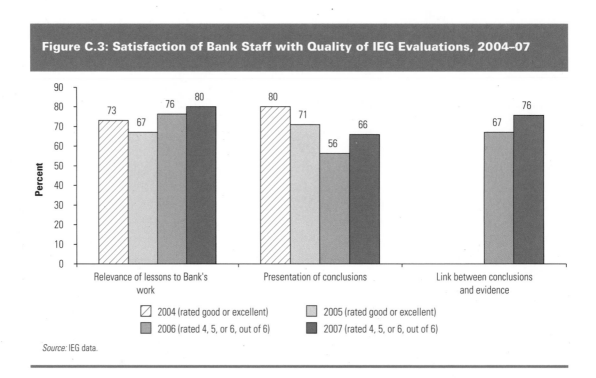

Figure C.3: Satisfaction of Bank Staff with Quality of IEG Evaluations, 2004–07

Source: IEG data.

in 2007, Executive Directors and advisor respondents were most satisfied with IEG's relevance to their work (with a mean of 4.95, 88 percent of respondents rating it 4 or higher). External respondents' satisfaction with IEG's quality was very high, with 89 percent of respondents rating all attributes of IEG's evaluations with a score of 4 or higher.

In response to the question of whether evaluations influenced their understanding of the subject area, 74 percent of Bank staff respondents rated it 4 or higher, a marked increase over 58 percent in 2006.[8] Ninety-four percent of Executive Directors and their advisors who responded rated this aspect at 4 or higher, compared with 90 percent in 2006. Among external respondents, 83 percent rated the influence of evaluations on their understanding of the subject area at 4 or higher, compared with 81 percent in 2006. At the more practical level of influencing Bank strategies and the design of results frameworks, Bank staff respondents rated IEG's influence a bit lower. On average, 58 percent rated these options at 4 or higher, with

means of 3.85 for IEG's influence on how outputs are linked to outcomes at the country level, and 3.96 for IEG's influence on sector strategies.

Use of evaluations for assessing the Bank's sector and country strategies is high among Executive Directors and their advisors, with more than 90 percent rating it at 4 or higher, and policies and procedures, with 87 percent assigning ratings of 4 or higher. Executive Directors and their advisors who responded use evaluations less for assessing Bank projects (73 percent rating it 4 or higher). Overall, Executive Director and advisor respondents made more use of IEG evaluations in 2007 than in 2006. The same holds true for Bank staff respondents, whose self-reported use has increased by 19 percent, on average, for all types of usage since 2006.[9] Bank staff respondents use evaluations mostly for commenting on the work of others, making a case for a particular course of action, and providing advice to clients, and less for modifying strategies or operations, or designing new projects or programs. However, in 2007, 45 percent of respondents rated use for modifying ongoing operations at 4

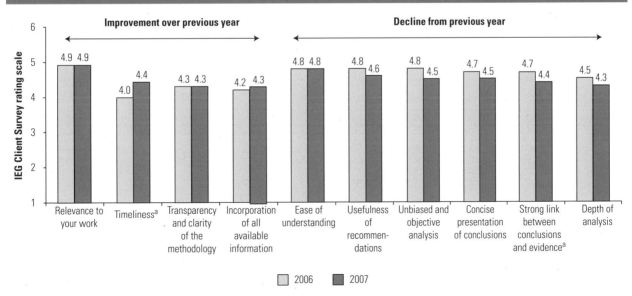

Figure C.4: Satisfaction of Executive Directors with Quality of IEG Evaluations

Source: IEG data.

Note: Bars show means on a six-point scale, where 1 = highly unsatisfied, and 6 = highly satisfied. Sample size for 2006 is 50, for 2007 is 58.

a. Difference is significant at 90 percent confidence level.

or higher, compared with only 27 percent in 2006. External clients use IEG evaluations mostly for research (76 percent), while 71 percent use it to refocus ongoing strategies or programs. Although use of evaluations was higher in 2007 than in 2006, respondents continued to point to obstacles to usefulness, such as the lack of specificity of recommendations to suggest how to put them into practice, and lack of reflection on the country context where the Bank operates, which would make findings relevant to Bank operations on the ground.

When asked about how to improve the evaluation for which they had been surveyed, 59 percent of staff respondents recommended that IEG make its findings more operational, compared with 57 percent in 2006. Broadening consultation with Bank staff was the second recommendation made by 47 percent of respondents (48 percent in 2006). This was followed by improving depth of analysis (2007: 41 percent; 2006: 45 percent) and broadening external consultation (2007: 40 percent; 2006: 35 percent). Executive Directors and their advisor respondents made similar suggestions, but 54 percent emphasized the importance of broadening external consultation more than consultation with Bank staff, which only 27 percent of respondents chose as a recommendation to IEG. External respondents' main recommendation was to broaden external consultation (59 percent), followed by more operational findings (51 percent) and obtaining more evidence (47 percent).

In 2007, the survey also included questions about the timeliness and relevance of four IEG quick products from 2006 and 2007. These were generally well received. Eighty-four percent of Bank staff and Executive Directors and advisor respondents rated them at 4 or higher on timeliness, and 80 percent rated them at 4 or higher on relevance. However, awareness of these notes was low, with senior management respondents (42 percent indicated no awareness with any of the four notes) and staff, whose awareness was below 40 percent for all but one note. Executive Directors and advisors who responded were generally well aware of these notes.

Communicating Knowledge from IEG Evaluations

Effective communication of IEG's knowledge to Bank staff, governments, other donors, and the international community is a crucial link between evaluations and outcomes. Over the last two years, IEG has undertaken extensive efforts to improve its outreach to Bank staff and the wider development community. After a series of pilot initiatives, IEG mainstreamed several new approaches on media outreach, e-mail marketing, Web promotions and an improved Help Desk, and successfully increased awareness among target audiences.

Awareness of evaluations, as reported by Bank staff who responded to the 2007 client survey, rose from 39 percent in 2004, to 61 percent in 2007. The number of follow-up inquiries to IEG's Help Desk increased tenfold during 2005 and has stayed at the same high level since, with about 2,400 inquiries each year. Help Desk inquiries are concerned with evaluation methodology, advice on M&E systems, and IEG's product portfolio, suggesting that IEG's outreach campaigns are triggering follow-up questions among key audience segments.

Over the past two years, IEG organized 11 media outreach campaigns to coincide with the release of its reports. These campaigns have produced extensive media coverage and generated an estimated 200 articles and reports in audiovisual media over the last two years.[10] The growing number of references in the media to IEG evaluations indicates strong interest in the Bank's performance on key development initiatives.

IEG's communication and outreach can be strengthened by providing more summaries of IEG findings. In the client surveys, about two-thirds of all client groups made this recommendation in both 2006 and 2007. Bank staff (39 percent of respondents) and Executive Directors and advisors (53 percent of respondents) continue to ask for more online accessibility to IEG content. Among external respondents, 60 percent asked for more training/education material. Forty percent of Executive Directors and advisor respondents made this recommendation as well. Going forward, IEG will work on its Web site, focusing on the development of new search tools that will make its content more accessible.

IEG Intermediate Outcomes: Evaluation Recommendations Incorporated into Bank Operations and Policy

IEG influences the Bank's effectiveness through recommendations to management as part of sector, thematic, and corporate evaluations, as well as Country Assistance Evaluations. Bank management is accountable to the Board for follow-up. One of the intermediate outcomes for IEG is the extent to which management incorporates IEG recommendations and findings in policy advice, program design, and project design (see box C.2).

The Management Action Record allows IEG to track its recommendations and to monitor the degree to which they have been adopted by management. The MAR tracks two indicators: the level of adoption[11] and the status of individual recommendations.[12] The MAR presents management's ratings on these two indicators and IEG's assessment of the same. The MAR includes IEG recommendations from the previous three calendar years.

The MAR for 2008 tracks management's progress on 57 recommendations. These include 22 new recommendations from the six IEG studies (excluding CAEs) presented to the Board in calendar year 2007, and 35 recommendations carried forward from calendar years 2005 and 2006.

The 2008 MAR shows a continuing high level of agreement from the Bank with IEG's recommendations. Of the 57 recommendations in the 2008 MAR, 96 percent (55 recommendations) have been accepted by Bank management,[13] similar to the rate of acceptance in earlier years (95 percent in MAR 2007 and MAR 2006).

In the 2008 MAR, as shown in figure C.5, IEG rated adoption medium or better for 95 percent of 52 recommendations. This compares with 85 percent (47 recommendations) in the 2007 MAR and 94 percent (72 recommendations) in the 2006 MAR. The share of recommendations adopted with substantial or high ratings was 42 percent in the 2008 MAR, down from 60 percent in the 2007 MAR. Therefore, the distribution of adoption ratings among the top three categories (medium, substantial, and high) has shifted toward medium.

The Bank's own assessment shows this shift and it is confirmed by IEG. In this regard, it is

---

Box C.2: Selected Impacts of IEG Evaluations

- The recently announced credit line to deal with catastrophes, such as earthquakes and hurricanes in MICs, directly reflects IEG's recommendation that a new mechanism be established to meet urgent needs in the early days of a disaster response.
- The Bank's recently promulgated strategy "Strengthening the World Bank's Rapid Response and Long-Term Engagement in Fragile States" responds directly to IEG's recommendation that internal Bank support for fragile states—including staff numbers, staff skills, guidance, and organizational incentives—needs to be strengthened.
- Prompted by IEG's primary education study and the accompanying volume of science-based sectoral knowledge, Bank projects more often now aim to measure learning outcomes, and, in particular, the reading fluency acquired in the early

grades. A major donor-financed workshop in March 2008 used findings and benchmarks identified by IEG.
- IEG's review of lines of credit led to a Bank-wide effort to identify and review their quality, sharing of experience among donors, and an Operations Policy and Country Services initiative to require early identification of lines of credit.
- IEG's evaluation of private sector development in the power sector contributed to a reassessment of the Bank's approach to infrastructure.
- The evaluation of social development fed directly into the preparation of the Bank's Social Development strategy.
- The global programs review resulted in greater scrutiny and streamlining of the Bank's approach to and governance of global programs.

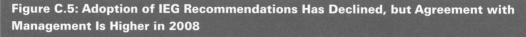

Figure C.5: Adoption of IEG Recommendations Has Declined, but Agreement with Management Is Higher in 2008

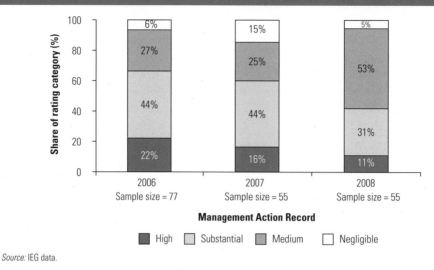

Source: IEG data.

noteworthy that agreement on adoption ratings between IEG and management was higher in 2008 than in previous years. IEG and management agreed on the rating on level of adoption for 65 percent of recommendations (36 out of 55).[14] And the disconnect between high and substantial adoption ratings by IEG and management was 18 percent (IEG rated 42 percent of recommendations high or substantial; management 60 percent) in 2008, compared with 28 percent in 2007 and 21 percent in 2006.

Going forward, the challenge is for IEG to continue producing high-quality evaluations with sensible and practical recommendations, retain the high level of agreement on those recommendations, and for the Bank to lift up its intensity of adoption and implementation.

Since 2006, recommendations that are older than three years are being retired from the MAR, subject to review by CODE and the Board.

IEG Intermediate Outcomes: Use of Evaluation Findings by Bank Staff at the Operational Level

IEG's performance on this intermediate outcome can be measured by whether Bank staff use IEG findings to improve Bank policy advice and program and project designs. The 2006 AROE found that IEG provides high-level knowledge that is useful for assessing programs, giving advice to clients, and making comments, but needs to focus on influencing ongoing and future operations. Focus groups conducted for that report showed that Task Team Leaders are least likely to report that they incorporate evaluation findings into planning and design. Their operational context requires information on how to conduct monitoring, establish indicators, and prepare projects for evaluation. Respondents in management positions reported greater use and usefulness of IEG products. CODE members rely heavily on IEG's reports, advice, and recommendations. These findings were also borne out in the 2007 client survey in which 72 percent of Bank staff respondents reported using IEG evaluations for making comments and giving advice to others. However, only 54 percent of staff report using evaluations for designing new operations, and 45 percent report using evaluations for modifying ongoing operations. Executive Directors and their advisors make heavy use of evaluations (90 percent indicating substantial use) for their oversight function of sector and country strategies, and Bank policies, but less so for project-level oversight (76 percent of respondents indicating substantial use).

To improve IEG's impact on Bank operations, IEG will need to continue giving greater emphasis to applied learning and real-time use of evaluation findings, to improve Bank performance. To meet this challenge, IEG needs to define its stance on engagement and learning with guidelines and funding for its staff. The more that operational staff are involved up front in the evaluation design and during the evaluation, the more likely the evaluation will deliver operationally relevant results and be geared toward learning. At the same time, close engagement challenges the evaluator's independence and might distract from the necessary accountability perspective. Finding the right balance and providing the proper incentives to IEG staff for engagement with operational staff during the evaluation and afterward for learning requires clear directions from IEG leadership.

Both the demand and supply features of GPGs can provide an obstacle to their provision. Individual countries "demand" GPGs only to the extent that this demand serves a national interest. Moreover, the features of different GPGs imply large variations in the manner through which a GPG should be supplied. This section provides a framework for considering how the Bank and the international community should arrange for the most efficient approach toward providing GPGs.

From the Demand Side

The extent of divergence between national and global benefit (or cost) of a GPG varies across a spectrum, and so the extent to which a particular good is truly a GPG is not always easy to assess precisely. Clean air provides a good example of a GPG. In contrast, some facets of communicable diseases are primarily national in scope, notwithstanding the fact that there may be other reasons why responses are supported by global partnerships.

This distinction is noteworthy. A country's perception of the divergence between national and global benefits and costs of GPGs influences whether a country "demands" a GPG and, therefore, whether there is action on the country level, the extent to which such engagement occurs, and the types of instruments that are used. For the Bank, the level of overlap between national and global net benefits can be one determinant of the type of role it can play in fostering GPGs, and the extent to which strategic intent is translated into action on the ground.

At one extreme, when the national benefits of the GPG coincide in large part with the benefits accruing to the global community (depicted in figure D.1), the Bank's country-based model can

work well to encourage countries to integrate the GPG into their national programs because the country's interests are already closely aligned with the worldwide interests. For example, a country will likely be more interested in controlling HIV/AIDS within its borders if it has a high HIV prevalence rate (and hence the health and social consequences are already felt at the national level). In such cases, the Bank should have influential national counterparts who are receptive to its support. In such circumstances, traditional Bank instruments such as IBRD and IDA lending can often be used.

At the other extreme, when the net benefits of the GPG are large at the dispersed global level but only minimally appropriable at the level of an individual nation state—as is the case for climate change—the Bank's country-based model may not be as useful because of that very divergence (depicted in figure D.2). In such instances, the

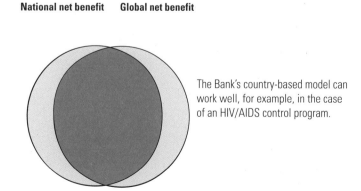

Figure D.1: Country Perception of Net Benefits When National and Global Interests Coincide

National net benefit   **Global net benefit**

The Bank's country-based model can work well, for example, in the case of an HIV/AIDS control program.

Source: IEG.

Figure D.2: Country Perception of Net Benefits When National and Global Interests Diverge

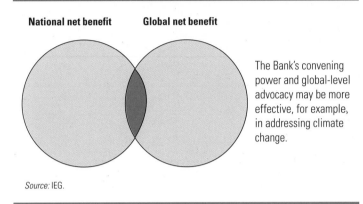

National net benefit   Global net benefit

The Bank's convening power and global-level advocacy may be more effective, for example, in addressing climate change.

Source: IEG.

Bank may be more successful in fostering GPGs by leveraging its convening power and providing constructive advocacy at the global level.

Between the two extremes, when there is some level of convergence in national and global net benefit, the Bank has a chance to prompt national action, but has to "push hard at the door." In fact there are several levers the Bank can use to, as it were, "push the circles together" and create a coincidence of national and global interest. Those levers include: (i) financing instruments; (ii) global programs, and (iii) advocacy—including convening power and support for international frameworks.

From the Supply Side

GPGs also have different features in the way they have to be supplied and this has implications for the way in which the Bank (and other bodies) deal with them. As shown in table D.1, some public goods are supplied through aggregate efforts, others by single best efforts. Some depend on the weakest link, others require coordination. These distinctions are important because they reveal different incentive challenges. While the desire of some countries to coordinate may be strong, the supply of public goods requiring an aggregate effort is usually prone to free riding. Supply of public goods requiring a single best effort can be easier to achieve than supply of a weakest-link public good, which can be undermined by a single failed state.

Table D.1: Bank Uses Different Vehicles to Support the Provision of Different Types of GPGs

	Supply-type of Global Public Good			
	Single best effort The action of a single actor or country (or small group of actors) provides a GPG. *For example, researchers in the United States developed two polio vaccines in the 1950s that were available to many other countries.*	**Weakest link** Inaction or a weak effort by a single country leads to undersupply of a GPG. *For example, the inability of a country to eradicate a communicable disease forces other countries to vaccinate against it.*	**Aggregate effort** A critical mass of countries each contributes individually to a GPG *For example, countries reduce or eliminate their production of ozone-depleting substances to preserve the global ozone layer.*	**Coordination** Countries act in harmony to jointly achieve an agreed upon GPG. *For example, countries agree to standards of measurement that facilitate international trade and cross-country comparisons*
Country-based interventions		**Crises and systemic risk** The Financial Sector Assessment Program helps countries identify vulnerabilities in their financial systems and determine needed reforms in order to avoid financial crises and potential global contagion.	**Climate change** The Carbon Fund mitigates against climate change through market-based mechanisms. The Global Environment Facility (GEF) fights climate change and protects biodiversity through grant finance.	
Advocacy and research	**Vaccines** The Global Alliance for Vaccines and Immunizations conducts research to provide new vaccines for communicable diseases that could then be shared with all countries. **Trade** The Bank's research and advocacy on trade provides pressure and evidence to encourage a prodevelopment Doha round of WTO negotiations.			**Avian influenza** The Bank conducted research that outlined the costs and benefits of avian influenza control, which served as an umbrella for international action.

World Bank-supported activity

Source: IEG.

Introduction

This year's Annual Review of Development Effectiveness (ARDE) tracks World Bank performance and examines a particular thematic topic, the Bank's work in fostering global public goods (GPGs). Management welcomes the new two-part format of the ARDE and considers the thematic topic timely and highly relevant. In Part I, the Bank's Independent Evaluation Group (IEG) reports on recent trends in the outcomes of Bank projects and country programs and analyzes progress in the quality and coverage of monitoring and evaluation (M&E) systems employed by the Bank. In Part II, IEG reviews the Bank's experience with (a) country-based support for client contributions to the supply of GPGs and (b) its advocacy for action on GPGs. This appendix provides brief responses to IEG's findings and suggestions in Part I and Part II, respectively.

Tracking Bank Performance

Management values the review of development outcomes and the Bank's M&E practice. IEG's feedback fosters learning from experience and is a factor in the medium-term improvement of Bank performance documented in the ARDE. Management agrees that the weakening of development outcomes in projects that exited the portfolio in fiscal 2007 warrants attention and outlines its actions below. Management also agrees with most of the suggestions to further improve the quality and coverage of M&E in projects, country programs, and global programs and partnerships (GPPs).

Project Outcomes

The ARDE confirms that the ratings for project outcomes have significantly improved over the medium term and have exceeded the Bank's performance benchmarks in each of the three years to end-fiscal 2007. Improvements have been particularly impressive in the Africa Region and in the water supply and sanitation sector. The report goes on to highlight and discuss two signs of weaknesses in the data for fiscal 2007, including a jump in the so-called disconnect— that is, the difference between the outcome ratings provided by Bank staff in the final Implementation Status and Results reports (ISRs) for ongoing projects and IEG's ratings in its reviews of the Bank's Implementation Completion and Results reports (ICRs)—and a decline in the share of projects with satisfactory outcomes, from a high of 83 percent in fiscal 2006 to 76 percent in fiscal 2007.

Actions in response to warning signals. Management concurs that a correct rating of likely outcomes in ongoing projects is necessary for its ability to take timely remedial action in problem projects, and that the fall in IEG exit ratings and the increased disconnect in fiscal 2007 must be recognized as a warning sign. This parallels findings under our more detailed review of IDA controls as well as QAG reports and the India detailed implementation review. Management is taking on these issues in the context of investment lending reform, notably changes in our supervision practices. As IEG notes, the more problematic areas are the noninfrastructure sectors and low-income countries (LICs), especially fragile states. Management is considering a more customized approach for implementation to reflect the complexities of these operational situations, moving beyond the traditional notion of supervision and incorporating the possibility of implementation support directed at capacity building. However, management is not waiting for the introduction of these reforms. Each Region has conducted its own review of ratings in ongoing operations. In the South Asia, East Asia and the Pacific, and Latin America and Caribbean Regions, Regional vice presidents have taken the lead in reviewing ISRs, with instructions for action by task teams. The Africa Region has adopted specific measures (involving country management, sector management, and the quality and knowledge services units) to reduce the disconnect, ensure realism in the ratings of ongoing operations, and strengthen accountability for project quality. In addition, the upcoming Development Policy Lending Retrospective will review the Bank's rating practice for development policy loan operations and, as necessary, will recommend appropriate actions to ensure that management receives timely information on weak performance in such operations.

Decline in fiscal 2007 project outcome ratings and increase in disconnect—some observations. Effective support for members' development efforts requires the Bank to take risks; consequently, not all the operations it supports will achieve the desired outcomes. Against this background, the share of Bank projects with a satisfactory development outcome in recent years has risen to a reasonable level—a level at which year-to-year variations are to be expected. However, management agrees that vigilance is warranted to ensure that the fiscal 2007 drop in ratings signifies a variation around that trend and not the beginning of a decline. IEG is to be commended for examining the possible impact of sample composition bias and of changes in the evaluation methodology on the fiscal 2007 outcomes, and for recalling key factors about which the Bank must always be vigilant, including poor or overly complex project design, articulation of overly ambitious expected outcomes, implementation delays, and weaknesses in project supervision and staff performance. In addition, management believes the following considerations to be pertinent.

- Reduced outcome ratings for development policy loans contribute to the reported overall drop in fiscal 2007 ratings. That reduction likely reflects in part the temporary impact of a recent decision to report on programmatic development policy loans only at the end of the series. As a result, for a few years, one-off development policy loans will make up a larger share of the sample for which outcome ratings are available. With programmatic development policy loans rated better than one-off development policy loans, on average, this shift in composition has an adverse, but likely transitory, effect on the average rating for the sample.

- Vigilance about "overly complex" project designs must not discourage staff from responding to client demand for sophisticated—and at times necessarily complex—products, particularly in middle-income countries (MICs). The risk of not achieving satisfactory outcomes may be higher in such circumstances, but taking that risk is necessary for the Bank's continued relevance to its members. The issue is not so much reducing complexity as it is having clear objectives and effective systems for tracking operational performance.

- In addressing task team performance, it is important to take into account the challenges that result from the Bank's commitment to increased harmonization and collaboration with development partners, particularly in LICs. Staff must devote more time to coordination and are generally more dependent on the actions of others for achieving results, notably pending greater harmonization around agreed results frameworks.

- The jump in the disconnect can in part be traced to the introduction of a new evaluation methodology in fiscal 2007, specifically to different paces of implementing the agreed rating system and rating criteria between IEG and the larger and more layered Bank operational complex. The ARDE estimates this effect as accounting for one percentage point of the jump in the disconnect, but it may have been higher. As more ISRs and ICRs apply the methodology already used in IEG's reviews, the divergence in ratings can be expected to decline.

Country Program Outcomes

The ARDE reports the average development outcome ratings for some two decades of country programs on the basis of IEG's Country Assistance Evaluations (CAEs), and, for more recent country programs (starting in fiscal 1999), on the basis of IEG's reviews of Country Assistance Strategy Completion Reports (CASCRs). The ARDE observes that in both sets, average outcomes for MIC programs surpass those for LIC programs by a considerable margin, and that higher outcome ratings for the more recent country programs—those for which CASCRs are available—reflect improvements in MIC programs only. It also compares average country program outcomes with average project outcomes and suggests that the lower rating for country program outcomes may indicate a failure of such programs to exploit synergies between the Bank's development services. Management offers two comments.

- The gap between the outcomes of MIC and LIC programs is a matter of concern to management. However, averages over long durations do not shed light on the underlying factors. Management encourages IEG to analyze changes in outcomes over time for subgroups of countries, with the analysis taking account of major changes, such as the introduction of CAS results frameworks and changes in evaluation methodology. Moreover, management wants to note that it has not yet introduced a standard rating methodology for CASCRs, and the methodology used by IEG self-initiated ratings of CASCRs has been evolving and has not yet been finalized.
- IEG's suggestion that lower outcome ratings for country programs than for projects indicate that country programs fail to exploit synergies among Bank development services is not substantiated in the report. The report acknowledges some of the factors that, in management's view, deprive the comparison of informative value (for example, different performance standards). Management notes that performance in country programs predating the introduction of CAS results frameworks in fiscal 2005 is measured against objectives that do not clearly distinguish between country outcomes and CAS program outcomes. As program outcomes come to reflect more realisti-

cally the Bank's role in supporting a country's development strategy, outcome ratings tend to improve. It is also important to recognize that CAS program outcomes can change during the CAS period as the Bank responds flexibly to changing client demand for its services.

Monitoring and Evaluation

The ARDE recognizes that as part of the results agenda the Bank has put in place strong policies and procedures for the monitoring and evaluation (M&E) of project and country program outcomes. For the projects and country programs reviewed, however, it reports a low quality of M&E and results frameworks. Management agrees with IEG's recommendations for improving the quality and use of M&E, including increased focus on providing good baseline information for project outcomes, articulating more clearly the link between project outputs and targeted outcomes, simplifying the CAS results frameworks, and using them not only for evaluation but also for program management. Ongoing efforts in the Regions to improve M&E are indeed focusing on these aspects, as is management in its reviews of proposed development policy loan operations and CASs. Management believes that the ARDE could have given more recognition to initiatives such as Regional M&E support for task teams, the development of scorecards in a number of countries, and greater use of M&E frameworks for management purposes (for example, for annual country portfolio performance reviews in the Latin America and the Caribbean Region). The ARDE might have also given greater recognition to the commitments and actions to date under the IDA14 and IDA15 Results Measurement Systems, notably in terms of baseline operational data.

Management does not share IEG's view that staff incentive problems continue to be a major obstacle to the improvement of M&E in projects and country programs; rather, it believes that the new policies and procedures and the ongoing efforts for enhancing practice are improving quality in the more recent projects and programs. It would have been appropriate in this regard to highlight the challenge of country capacity for results management, since lack of data in poorer countries often is the most important obstacle to improving M&E frameworks. Helping partner countries overcome these data problems is a Bank priority, notably through the Marrakech Action Plan for Statistics, the framework discussed by the Board in May 2006. While this is a long-term effort, there has been progress. A key target of this plan is to help all low-income countries develop a national strategy for improving their statistical system. All but one Sub-Saharan African country (Somalia) have a strategy or are working on one. The Bank's multidonor Trust Fund for Statistical Capacity Building has provided 20 new grants to countries for strategy preparation since 2006. Following the Third International Roundtable on Managing for Development Results, in Hanoi, staff have been working closely with other development partners through the Partnership for Statistics for Development in the 21st Century to find the resources to scale up the implementation of these strategies. Part of the effort is mainstreaming statistical capacity building in country operations. New statistical capacity-building (STATCAP) lending projects have been approved for Kenya and Russia, and pipeline countries include Bolivia, Tanzania, and India. Two donors—the Netherlands and the United Kingdom—are working with the Bank to establish a new Statistics for Results Facility, which will promote better coordinated efforts by donors at the country level, and will provide grants to help finance the implementation of national statistical improvement plans and link them more closely with national development strategies. Staff are working to launch this facility in Ghana at the forthcoming High-Level Forum on Aid Effectiveness.

In discussing the M&E of projects and country programs reviewed, the ARDE could have paid more attention to an obvious legacy effect. The large majority of projects reviewed were approved prior to the adoption of the new policies and procedures; and nearly all results-based CASs reviewed were from the first round, in which results came from an existing portfolio of operations that had been approved prior to

that date. As noted in the report, in the small sample of reviewed projects approved since fiscal 2005, the share of projects with substantial or high M&E quality doubled. As more IEG reviews of results-based CASs from the second round become available, the ratings for the quality of results frameworks are likely to improve as well.

Management finds the ARDE's review of experience with the Bank's impact evaluations helpful and agrees that their increased use is important for strengthening the knowledge base for reporting on the Bank's corporate results; however, management is also aware of practical barriers to impact evaluation work in the context of specific operations. Management concurs with the emphasis in the report on strengthening results reporting at the corporate level. It recently proposed to prepare a Bankwide results report that will provide an overview of results achieved through Bank activities and report on progress in the Bank's results focus and measurement systems.

Shared Global Challenges

The ARDE reviews the Bank's experience with country program support for GPGs and offers a number of recommendations on bridging the gap between global needs and country preferences. It also reviews the Bank's advocacy work on GPGs.

Country-Based Support for GPGs

Management welcomes the report's many valuable insights into the challenges of supporting countries' contributions in cases where global and country interests diverge significantly and international agreement on a course of collective action has not yet been reached. Management also appreciates the careful review of the Bank's work on the country level—in the context of country programs and through country-level activities of global programs and partnerships—and the proposals for strengthening that work. Management agrees with many of the observations and assessments. Some, however, require comments, notably those on the extent of Bank involvement on the country level, the Bank's ability to provide attractive financial support for the GPG efforts of MICs, the reliance on the country program model, the attention paid to fostering GPGs in country and regional strategies, the deployment of global programs, and the option of setting aside corporate administrative funds for high priority GPG work at the country level.

Bank involvement in GPGs at the country level. The ARDE observes that GPGs other than environmental commons are not sufficiently emphasized in CASs and that the extent of Bank involvement in GPG issues varies widely among countries. This observation fails to take into account the framework for such Bank involvement.[1] Since the Bank is only one player among many, the framework calls for identifying where there is a gap not being met by other agencies and then filling the gap in areas where the Bank has the capability and a comparative advantage. At the country level, country ownership and response to client demand is the primary principle of Bank involvement—that is, the Bank works with clients on issues of global or regional concern and supports their efforts at addressing such issues. In sum, the appropriate role for the Bank at the country level is situation-specific to the GPG being supported and to the country context; hence, variations in the extent of Bank involvement at the country level among GPGs and among countries are to be expected. For example, on communicable diseases, substantial funding is flowing from large vertical funds. Here the challenge is to ensure that the funding is balanced by Bank support for health sector systems and other government priorities for the delivery of health services. While not presented in CASs as support for a global public good, such support by the Bank is key for bridging the gap between global and country interests in the area of communicable diseases (that is, it provides indirect support to the respective GPG). Regarding climate change, pending a future global climate agreement, country ownership and an effective country support program can be built only on demonstrated development opportunities and advantages of a low-carbon, climate-resilient strategy tailored to specific country circumstances.

Financial support for MICs' contributions to GPGs. The ARDE presents ample evidence of the effectiveness of concessional finance in bridging gaps between global needs and country preferences in International Development Association-eligible countries. With respect to International Bank for Reconstruction and Development (IBRD)-eligible countries, the report recognizes the Global Environment Facility (GEF) as a source of concessional financing and carbon finance as an innovative mechanism the Bank can deploy also in MICs. But the report pays insufficient attention to the Bank's ability to further mobilize and innovate finance for scaling-up action on climate change, in cooperation with development partners and the private sector, and it also neglects the possible leveraging of IBRD and International Finance Corporation financing and risk management services through blending with concessional donor funds. Management considers overly pessimistic the report's conclusion with respect to future Bank work on GPGs in MICs that ". . . the Bank has not been able to call on an attractive large-scale funding program . . . to encourage comprehensive action on climate change." Given that the World Bank Group only recently began full-fledged efforts to step up climate action to scale, the conclusion appears premature. For example, the Bank works with donor countries to mobilize some $5 billion in new and additional financing for the proposed Clean Technology Fund, with the expectation that these new resources will leverage another $25–30 billion in financing for low-carbon investments.

Use of the country program model. Management is aware that country-based work on GPGs faces challenges in cases where global and country interests diverge and there is no international framework for collective action, but it believes that such challenges can be addressed. Management does not agree with the report's broad conclusion that relying on the country program model for the Bank's work on GPGs is a "double-edged sword." The Bank's ultimate clients are poor people. Using the country program model, the Bank is better able to provide analysis that puts growth and poverty reduction at the core and relates GPG challenges to this goal. Importantly, using the country program model also helps ensure country ownership of the actions supported by the Bank. These considerations argue for integrating the country-level activities of GPPs into country programs and against allowing them to bypass country programs. The example of Ethiopia's health budget, which due to the proliferation of vertical health funds devotes some 50 percent of resources to HIV/AIDS, is instructive. That the Bank can balance resource flows by targeting its resources to other health needs in the country is a considerable strength of the country program model. The key challenge, in management's view, is to more thoroughly integrate GPGs into the diagnosis of countries' development challenges and the dialogue with the government as part of the CAS process. With this analysis in place, the appropriate contribution of global programs and trust funds as part of the CAS support program can then be determined, consistent with the plans by vice-presidential units for implementation of the Trust Fund Management Framework.

Country and regional strategies. The report provides valuable information on the treatment of GPGs in CASs, Regional strategies, sector strategies, and Bankwide strategy documents. In light of recent developments, however, management finds too categorical the general statement in the report that the Bank's attention to GPGs ". . . wanes as one moves down from corporate strategies to sector or regional strategies, and then down one level further to country strategies." For example, the 2008 Latin America and Caribbean Regional strategy update emphasizes support for clients' efforts to address global issues, and this priority is translated into specific actions planned in the recent round of CASs, including those for Brazil, Colombia, and Mexico. (In March 2008, the Board approved a $500 million loan to Mexico to support implementation of its National Climate Change Action Plan.)

Global programs. The report shows that there is room for improvement in deploying global and regional programs at the country level. Manage-ment welcomes the report's proposal to strengthen M&E quality in GPPs, though it notes that an M&E framework for Development Grant Facility-supported global programs is in place and the Consultative Group on International Agriculture Research program offers an example of good practice. Management appreciates IEG's insight into factors influencing the integration of global program activities into country operations, notably the strong positive effect of substantial developing country representation in the governing body of a GPP in both enhancing legitimacy and fostering stronger linkages with country operations. But management also believes that the report should more clearly distinguish among subsets of GPPs (instead of treating GPPs as if they are all interchangeably applicable at the country level or all deal with GPG issues) and should also recognize that the Bank's role at the country level is limited in GPPs where the Bank is not an implementing agency. Management agrees that better integration of global funds at the country level is important. To that end, over the last two years, the Bank has been working closely with the Development Assistance Committee of the Organisation for Economic Co-operation and Development and with bilateral donors and partner countries on an initiative to better align global programs with country operations. This initiative has contributed to preparations for the Accra High-Level Meeting.

Strengthening country program support for GPGs. Management agrees with the report's suggestions for strengthening the Bank's country-based support for GPGs, notably through improved organizational arrangements to coordinate global, regional, and national activities; better delivery of the Bank's global knowledge to country teams and improved deployment of network anchor experts; support for clients' efforts to gain greater voice in shaping responses to global issues; and the exercise of greater selectivity in the Bank's engagement in global programs. Management agrees on the desirability of strengthening incentives to deliver GPGs at the country level where that is appropriate, but has reservations about the suggested option of setting aside significant administrative funding at the corporate level for allocation to high-priority GPG work at the country level. This could distort incentives and encourage supply-driven initiatives. A more effective approach—as already demonstrated in the Latin American and Caribbean Region—is Regional management commitment and clear guidance to staff on the need to be attuned to client demands for support for their GPG priorities. There also needs to be an ongoing dialogue among the networks and Regions on staffing and resource allocation, to address key corporate priorities through country operations where there is demand at the country level. This would be strengthened by recognition in staff performance evaluations, as indicated in the report.

Advocacy on GPGs

Management appreciates IEG's thoughtful analysis of the Bank's successful advocacy work on GPGs and its achievements in creating innovative financing mechanisms. Management agrees with most of the assessments, though it believes that the report could have provided more recognition to the Bank's performance in preserving biodiversity, with funding from the GEF and own Bank resources. Two comments are warranted.

- The report acknowledges the Bank's many activities in support of the international climate change agenda, including securing resources for the GEF (the financial mechanism of the United Nations Framework Convention on Climate Change), developing methodologies to put the Kyoto Protocol's Clean Development Mechanism into action, launching carbon funds, and supporting the demonstration, deployment, and transfer of low-carbon technologies and adaptation technologies. In this light, management believes that the report's summary assessment that ". . . the extent to which the Bank has been a leading influential

advocate on climate change is more debatable" does not fully reflect this reality.

- Management agrees that increased Bank efforts are merited to strengthen the voice and representation of developing countries in the governance of global programs. For example, the participation of developing countries in the design of the Climate Investment Funds, including the design of a governance structure with equal representation of donor and recipient countries, has been critical to providing legitimacy for these funds. This participation is essential to set the stage at the global level for climate change mitigation programs at the country level.

Conclusion

This year's ARDE has again provided a valuable service by tracking development outcomes and improvements in M&E frameworks, a service that helps the Bank improve its performance. Management commends IEG for an insightful review of the Bank's experience with fostering global public goods through support for countries' efforts and through constructive advocacy. In its lessons of experience, the report appropriately focuses on ways to strengthen the Bank's country-level support for GPGs. As detailed above, management generally agrees with the report's suggestions, although it has reservations about the option of setting aside administrative funding at the corporate level earmarked for country-level GPG work. But management also stresses the need for clarity on the Bank's role in supporting a country's efforts at addressing issues of global or regional concern. Such support must build on the Bank's core mandate to foster the country's growth and poverty reduction goals, support measures that are owned by the country, and take into account, for each GPG, the involvement of other agencies and partners and the Bank's capability and comparative advantage.

Chapter 1

1. Until this year, IEG produced an Annual Review of Operations Evaluation (AROE), which included analysis of the Bank's monitoring and evaluation systems, as well as an IEG self-evaluation. In consultation with CODE, the AROE and ARDE have been combined this year into a single document that maintains the essential features of both.

Chapter 2

1. See, for instance, Wappenhans (1992) for an early critique of this "lending culture."

2. IEG's measure of *outcome* considers three factors; relevance, efficacy, and efficiency. *Relevance* measures the expected development impact of a project design by weighing the continuing relevance of a project's objectives. *Efficacy* refers to the extent to which each objective was achieved, or expected to be achieved. *Efficiency* measures the cost-effectiveness of a project, based mainly on sectorwide best practices and indicators where available. Combining these three factors, overall outcome is rated on a 6-point scale, ranging from highly satisfactory to highly unsatisfactory.

3. IEG's *sustainability* measure assesses the resilience to risk of net benefit flows over time by answering the following questions: At the time of evaluation, what is the resilience to risks affecting future net benefit flows? How sensitive is the intervention to changes in the operating environment? Will the intervention continue to produce net benefits as long as intended, or even longer? How well will the intervention weather shocks and changing circumstances?

4. Under the new harmonized evaluation criteria for project evaluations, approved in October 2005, projects would no longer be rated for their sustainability and institutional development impact. Therefore, the fiscal 2003–07 cohort includes about 50 percent of evaluated fiscal 2006 projects, and seven projects in fiscal 2007.

5. The analysis excludes the sector boards on gender, global information and technology, poverty reduction, and social development because IEG has evaluated very few projects managed by these sector boards.

6. Data for fiscal 2007 remains partial because only three-quarters of the projects that closed in fiscal 2007 have been evaluated to date.

7. During implementation, the Bank manages a project by means of an ongoing Implementation Status and Results report (ISR). Upon completion of a project, the Bank conducts a self-evaluation. This self-evaluation is called an Implementation Completion and Results report (ICR), which is then independently evaluated by IEG, leading to an Implementation Completion and Results review.

8. Project outcomes have also declined when weighted by disbursements, from 90 percent of projects rated moderately satisfactory or better in fiscal 2006, to 83 percent in fiscal 2007.

9. IEG, in agreement with the Bank, introduced an explicit requirement for evidence to substantiate assessments of performance in projects, which fully went into effect at the beginning of fiscal 2007.

10. CASCR reviews tend to assess a shorter time-frame for the period of a single CAS, generally between 3 and 5 years. Country Assistance Evaluations (CAEs) assess Bank programs over a longer period, typically between 6 and 10 years, and involve an in-depth mission to the country. This analysis draws on IEG reviews of 59 CASCRs completed since fiscal 2004, and one CASCR completed near the end of fiscal 2003.

Chapter 3

1. Prior to 2004, the Bank required log-frames in their projects. The results framework places greater emphasis on the outcomes, differentiating between the final outcomes (the project development objec-

tives) and intermediate outcomes, which can be used to monitor progress toward achieving the project development objectives. The log-frame included inputs and outputs as well as outcomes.

2. An M&E system with a "high" rating is expected to strongly influence project performance, provide sufficient information to satisfactorily assess the stated project objectives, and contribute to testing the underlying development model (or results chain). Conversely, a system rated "negligible" would have many weaknesses, have very little impact on the project or program, be insufficient to satisfactorily assess the stated project objectives, and contribute little to testing the development model.

3. As of February 2008.

4. BP 2.11, *Country Assistance Strategies,* was updated in June 2005 to reflect the results-based CAS approach.

5. Data on Bank-supported evaluations were drawn from the Development Impact Evaluation database, May 13, 2008.

Chapter 6

1. In-person and telephone interviews of 23 World Bank operational managers, including country and sector directors.

2. The "successor" to the CAS—the Country Partnership Strategy (CPS)—is used in more recent cases. All references here to CASs, therefore, also cover CPSs.

3. In-person and telephone interviews of 23 World Bank operational managers, including country and sector directors.

4. Discussed by the Executive Board in May 2008.

5. Such as the World Bank's sustainable development strategy: *Making Sustainable Commitments: An Environment Strategy for the World Bank. 2001.*

6. With the exception of the East Asia and Pacific and the Europe and Central Asia environment strategies, which have a strong focus on GPGs.

7. The Health, Nutrition, and Population strategy, although it mentions the promotion of GPGs, provides very little detail on its GPG strategy.

8. Here GPGs are defined to include all work on the following Bank-defined themes: HIV/AIDS, other communicable diseases, biodiversity, climate change, water resources management, other environment and natural resources management, international financial architecture, regional integration, trade facilitation and market access, and other trade and integration.

9. Estimates are drawn from the Global Public Goods Working Group.

10. In-person and telephone interviews of 23 World Bank operational managers, including country and sector directors.

11. In-person and telephone interviews of 23 World Bank operational managers, including country and sector directors.

12. Information from Avian Flu Resources by World Bank Operations Policy and Country Services (OPCS).

13. It should be noted that this estimate covers all Bank-supported trade projects, a significant share of which were directed at domestic trade issues, as opposed to the global dimension of trade.

14. For shorthand, this section uses the term "global programs," and the points made largely refer also to regional programs, unless otherwise stated.

15. Here the GPGs included fall under four of the Bank's five GPG areas, excluding creation and sharing of knowledge.

16. Findings from an IEG focus group conducted with eight Task Team Leaders from Global and Regional Partnership Programs directly involved with global public goods, April 2, 2008.

Chapter 7

1. *Making Trade Work for Poor People* (Stern 2002) was considered a timely input to the Doha Trade Ministerial, and *Global Economic Prospects 2004: Realizing the Development Promise of the Doha Agenda* (World Bank 2004c) was published ahead of the Cancun Trade Ministerial. World Trade Organization members cited these sources as contributing to their understanding of the issues and to the debate (IEG 2006a).

2. The Deaton report (2006), which evaluated the Bank's research program from 1998 to 2005, noted that "historically, the Bank has had a very active, vibrant and influential research program on international trade and trade policy . . . [although] suspects that it has not been as influential in recent years as once was the case."

3. For instance, the World Bank's position on trade policy—including pressuring the United States and Europe to reduce agricultural subsidies—was widely reported in the popular press, including nearly 50 references in the *Economist* and the *Financial Times* since January 2005. World Bank (2006a) discusses the effectiveness of these public interventions more fully.

4. For example, an op-ed piece in the *Financial Times* at the time of the Bali conference, late 2007.

5. Barrett (2006) shows that the incentives for cooperation in R&D depend on the prospects of the technologies embodying R&D being diffused. If new technologies are diffused to developing countries, rich countries will have greater incentive to finance R&D.

6. Refer to the following on CGIAR's Web site at www.cgiar.org: "Research & Impact," "CGIAR on Global Issues," "Global Climate Change: Can Agriculture Cope?"; and the World Bank's Web site on "Climate Change Research: Sustainable Rural and Urban Development" at http://go.worldbank.org/7Q6I1HUPZ0.

7. In-person and telephone interviews of 11 senior experts from international institutions, international NGOs, partner countries, and the World Bank.

8. This is in part because loans tend to be slower in disbursing, and the program is still very new.

9. In detail, those roles are: lender, founder, member of the governing body, convener, financial contributor, trust-fund trustee, house secretariat, implementing agency, chair of the governing body, trust-fund manager, and cosponsor (IEG 2004b).

10. Development Committee Communiqué, April 13, 2008.

Appendix A

1. IEG's *institutional development impact* measure evaluates the extent to which an intervention improves the ability of a country or region to make more efficient, equitable, and sustainable use of its human, financial, and natural resources. Such improvements can derive from changes in values, customs, laws and regulations, and organizational mandates.

2. The analysis excludes the sector boards on gender, global information and technology, poverty reduction, and social development.

3. The five countries/areas that received Special Financing Grants in the past decade are Bosnia and Herzegovina, Kosovo, Serbia, Timor-Leste, and the West Bank and Gaza.

4. Of this amount, $351 million financed operations in the West Bank and Gaza.

Appendix C

1. Mandate of the Director-General, Evaluation.

2. IEG's independence has been validated according to the standards of the OECD's Development Assistance Committee and the U.S. Government Accountability Office (among others), as documented in two papers: IEG, "OED Reach: Independence of OED," Feb-

ruary 23, 2003; and "2004 External Review of OED" on IEG's Web site at www.worldbank.org/ieg/intro.

3. The Bank's new framework for global public goods (World Bank 2007d) makes explicit reference to IEG's evaluation of regional programs as the foundation for expanding the Bank's work in regional programs.

4. Good examples for a CASCR and CASCR Review are the Philippines CASCR from April 2005 and IEG's review from May 2005, and the Yemen CASCR from May 2006 and IEG's review from June 2006. These CASCRs won IEG 2006 and 2007 Good Practice Awards.

5. Going forward, CASCR ratings will become a tier 2 indicator in the IDA15 Results Measurement System.

6. The award categories are Projects, Implementation Completion and Results reports, Country Programs, Country Assistance Strategy Completion Reports, Monitoring and Evaluation, and Initiatives with Demonstrated Impact/Results.

7. Although 24 percent is not a high response rate, a comparison of respondent and nonrespondent characteristics (grade level, region, headquarters/country office) shows that both groups are very similar. The only dimension with a difference of more than 6 percent between respondents and nonrespondents is the share of headquarters and country office staff.

8. It should be noted that this question included a "not applicable" answer option in 2007, but not in 2006. The percentages presented in the text include these responses in the denominator.

9. Previous note applies.

10. This compares with about seven reports about IEG in the media each year between 1996 and 2004. The IEG reports with the highest coverage were evaluation of Bank assistance to middle-income countries, from 2007, and the evaluation of Bank assistance to fragile states, from 2006. For both reports, IEG undertook multiple media launches in Washington, D.C. and in the field.

11. Level of adoption ratings are *high*—fully adopted; *substantial*—largely adopted but not fully incorporated into policy, strategy, or operations as yet; *medium*—adopted in some operational and policy work but not to a significant degree in key areas; and *negligible*—no evidence or plan for adoption, or plans and actions for adoption are in a very preliminary stage.

12. The status of recommendations is rated as: *active* and remains actionable by management; *complete* and archived in the e-MAR; *obsolete* or overtaken by

events and archived in e-MAR; *difference of opinion* between management and IEG.

13 . Recommendations that were not accepted by management will be excluded from the following data analysis.

14. This excludes the four recommendations on which there was a difference of opinion between IEG and management. These did not receive an adoption rating and are excluded from the sample when comparing levels of adoption.

Appendix E

1. See World Bank 2007m.

Baer, Paul, Tom Athanasiou, and Sivan Kartha. 2007. *The Right to Development in a Climate Constrained World: The Greenhouse Development Rights Framework*. Heinrich Böll Stiftung Publications on Ecology. Berlin: Heinrich Böll Foundation.

Barrett, Scott. 2006. "Climate Treaties and 'Breakthrough' Technologies." *American Economic Review: Papers and Proceedings* 96 (2): 22–25.

———. 2007. *Why Cooperate? The Incentive to Supply Global Public Goods*. New York: Oxford University Press.

———. 2008. "The World Bank's Role in Fostering Global Public Goods: Climate Change and Essential Medicines." ARDE background paper. Available on this evaluation's Web site at www.worldbank.org/ieg.

Benedick, R.E. 1998. *Ozone Diplomacy: New Directions in Safeguarding the Planet*. Cambridge, MA: Harvard University Press.

Brahmbhatt, Milan. 2005. "Avian and Human Pandemic Influenza—Economic and Social Impacts." Speech delivered during the "Global Partners Meeting on Avian Influenza and Human Pandemic Influenza," hosted by the World Health Organization, Geneva, Switzerland, November 7–9.

CAN-E (Climate Action Network Europe). 2002. "CAN Europe Comments on PCF Plantar Project." May 7. Brussels: CAN-E. http://www.climnet.org/pubs/CANEuropePlantar.pdf.

Carr, Christopher, and Flavia Rosembuj. 2007 "World Bank Experiences in Contracting for Emission Reductions." *Environmental Liability*, No. 2.

Deaton, Angus, Abhijit Banerjee, Nora Lustig, and Ken Rogoff. 2006. *An Evaluation of World Bank Research, 1998–2005*. Washington, DC: World Bank.

Ellis, Jane, and Sami Kamel. 2007. "Overcoming Barriers to Clean Development Mechanism Projects." Organisation for Economic Co-operation and Development and International Energy Agency. Paris: OECD. http://cd4cdm.org/Publications/Overcoming BarriersCDMprojects.pdf.

GLCA (Global Leadership for Climate Action). 2007. Framework for a Post-2012 Agreement on Climate Change. http://www.unfoundation.org/files/pdf/2007/GLCA_Framework2007.pdf.

House of Commons—International Development Committee. 2008. "DFID and the World Bank: Sixth Report of Session 2007–08," Vol. 1. London, UK: House of Commons.

IEG (Independent Evaluation Group). 2002. *The World Bank's Approach to Global Programs: An Independent Evaluation*. Phase 1, Report No. 26284-GLB. Washington, DC: World Bank.

———. 2004a. *Annual Report on Operations Evaluation*. IEG Study Series. Washington, DC: World Bank.

———. 2004b. *Addressing the Challenges of Globalization: An Independent Evaluation of the World Bank's Approach to Global Programs*. IEG Study Series. Washington, DC: World Bank.

———. 2004c. *The CGIAR at 31—An Independent Meta-Evaluation of the Consultative Group on International Agricultural Research*. Washington, DC: World Bank.

———. 2005. *Committing to Results: Improving the Effectiveness of HIV/AIDS Assistance*. IEG Study Series. Washington, DC: World Bank.

———. 2006a. *Assessing World Bank Support for Trade (1987–2004): An IEG Evaluation*. IEG Study Series. Washington, DC: World Bank.

———. 2006b. *Hazards of Nature, Risks to Development: An IEG Evaluation of World Bank Assistance for Natural Disasters*. Washington, DC: World Bank.

———. 2006c. *Annual Review of Development Effectiveness: Getting Results*. Washington, DC: World Bank.

———. 2006d. *Annual Report on Operations Evaluation*. IEG Study Series. Washington, DC: World Bank.

————. 2006e. *Engaging with Fragile States: An IEG Review of World Bank Support to Low-Income Countries under Stress.* Washington, DC: World Bank.

————. 2007a. *Development Results in Middle-Income Countries: An Evaluation of the World Bank's Support.* Washington, DC: World Bank.

————. 2007b. *Sourcebook for Evaluating Global and Regional Partnership Programs: Indicative Principles and Standards.* Washington, DC: World Bank.

————. 2007c. *The Development Potential of Regional Programs: An Evaluation of World Bank Support of Multicountry Operations.* Washington, DC: World Bank.

————. 2007d. *World Bank Assistance to Agriculture in Sub-Saharan Africa: An IEG Review.* Washington, DC: World Bank.

————. 2008a. *Supporting Environmental Sustainability: An Evaluation of World Bank Group Experience, 1990–2007.* IEG Study Series. Washington, DC: World Bank.

————. 2008b. *Progress Report on IEG's Activities Relating to Global and Regional Partnership Programs.* CODE Subcommittee Discussion Paper. Washington, DC: World Bank.

————. 2008c. *Public Sector Reform: What Works and Why?: An IEG Evaluation of World Bank Support.* Washington, DC: World Bank.

————. 2008d. *Using Training to Build Capacity for Development: An Evaluation of Project-Based and WBI Training.* IEG Study Series. Washington, DC: World Bank.

ITF (International Task Force on Global Public Goods). 2006. *Meeting Global Challenges: International Cooperation in the National Interest.* Final report. Stockholm: ITF.

Kaul, Inge, Isabelle Grunberg, and Marc Stern, eds. 1999. *Global Public Goods: International Cooperation in the 21st Century.* New York: Oxford University Press.

Müller, Benito, and Harald Winkler. 2008. "One Step Forward, Two Steps Back? The Governance of the World Bank Climate Investment Funds." Energy and Environment Comment. February. Oxford, UK: Oxford Institute for Energy Studies. http://www.oxfordenergy.org/pdfs/comment_0208-1.pdf.

Osterholm, Michael. 2007. "Unprepared for a Pandemic (H5N1 avian influenza virus)." *Foreign Affairs* 86 (2): 47–57.

Redman, Janet. 2008. *World Bank: Climate Profiteer.* Washington, DC: Institute for Policy Studies.

http://www.ips-dc.org/reports/#292.

Rodrik, Dani. 2006. "Goodbye Washington Consensus, Hello Washington Confusion? A Review of the World Bank's Economic Growth in the 1990s: Learning from a Decade of Reform." *Journal of Economic Literature* 44 (4): 973–87.

Schneider, Lambert. 2007. *Is the CDM Fulfilling Its Environmental and Sustainable Development Objectives?: An Evaluation of the CDM and Options for Improvement.* Report prepared for the World Wildlife Fund. November 5. Berlin: World Wildlife Fund. http://www.wwf.org.uk/filelibrary/pdf/cdm_fill_objectives.pdf

Smith, Richard, David Woodward, Arnab Acharya, and Robert Beaglehole. 2004. "Communicable Disease Control: A 'Global Public Good' Perspective." *Health Policy and Planning* 19 (5): 271–78,

Stern, Nicholas 2002. "Making Trade Work for Poor People." Speech delivered at the National Council of Applied Economic Research, New Delhi, November 28. http://siteresources.worldbank.org/INTRES/Resources/stern_speech_makingtrworkforpoor_nov2002.pdf

————. 2006. *The Economics of Climate Change: The Stern Review.* Cabinet Office, Her Majesty's Treasury, United Kingdom.

Sweden Ministry for Foreign Affairs. 2001. *Financing and Providing Global Public Goods: Expectations and Prospects. Study 2001:2.* Prepared by Francisco Sagasti and Keith Bezanson, on behalf of the Institute of Development Studies, Sussex, U.K.; Stockholm, Sweden.

UNSIC (United Nations System Influenza Coordinator) and World Bank. 2007. *Responses to Avian Influenza and State of Pandemic Readiness: Third Global Progress Report.* New York: UNSIC-World Bank.

Wappenhans, W.A. 1992. *Report of the Portfolio Management Task Force.* World Bank, Washington, DC.

Wheeler. David. 2008. "Crossroads at Mmamabula: Will the World Bank Choose the Clean Energy Path?" Working Paper No. 140. Center for Global Development, Washington, DC.

Woods, Ngaire. Forthcoming. "Governance Matters: The IMF and Sub-Saharan Africa." In *Finance, Development, and the IMF,* ed. James Boughton and Domenico Lombardi. Oxford, UK: Oxford University Press.

Woods, Ngaire, and Domenico Lombardi. 2006. "Uneven Patterns of Governance: How Developing Countries

Are Represented at the IMF." *Review of International Political Economy* 13 (3): 480–515.

World Bank. 1997. "Toward Global Sustainability," James D. Wolfensohn's speech to the United Nations General Assembly Special Session on the Environment, New York, June 25.

———. 2000. *Report of the Working Group on Improving Quality of Monitoring and Evaluation in Bank Financed Operations.* Operations Policy and Country Services Department. Washington, DC: World Bank.

———. 2001. *Making Sustainable Commitments: An Environment Strategy for the World Bank.* Washington, DC: World Bank.

———. 2003a. *Country Assistance Strategies: Retrospective and Future Directions (CAS Retro III).* Operations Policy and Country Services Department. Washington, DC: World Bank.

———. 2003b. *Putting Our Commitments to Work: An Environment Strategy Implementation Progress Report.* Washington, DC: World Bank.

———. 2004a. "OP/BP 8.60, Development Policy Lending." Operations Policy and Country Services Department. World Bank, Washington, DC.

———. *2004b. Responding to Climate Change: Proposed Action Plan for the World Bank in Latin America.* Washington, DC: World Bank.

———. *2004c. Global Economic Prospects 2004: Realizing the Development Promise of the Doha Agenda.* Washington, DC: World Bank.

———. 2005a. *Results Focus in Country Assistance Strategies: A Stock Taking of Results-Based CASs.* Operations Policy and Country Services Department. Washington, DC: World Bank.

———. 2005b. *Harmonized Evaluation Criteria for ICR and OED Evaluations. OPCS Guidelines.* Operations Policy and Country Services Department. Washington, DC: World Bank.

———. 2005c. *Improving Health, Nutrition, and Population Outcomes in Sub-Saharan Africa: The Role of the World Bank.* Washington, DC: World Bank.

———. 2005d. "Program Framework Document for Proposed Loans/Credits/Grants in the Amount of US$500 Million Equivalent for a Global Program for Avian Influenza Control and Human Pandemic Preparedness and Response." Report No. 34386. Washington, DC: World Bank.

———. 2006a. "Strengthening the World Bank's Engagement with IBRD Partner Countries, Development Committee." Report No. DC2006-0014, World Bank, Washington, DC.

———. 2006b. "Avian and Human Influenza: Financing Needs and Gaps." Technical note prepared for the International Pledging Conference on "Avian and Human Influenza," in Beijing, China, January 17–18.

———. 2006c. "Avian and Human Influenza: Multi-Donor Financing Framework." Technical note prepared for the International Pledging Conference on "Avian and Human Influenza," in Beijing, China, January 17–18.

———. 2006d. *Forest Carbon Partnership Facility: A Framework for Piloting Activities to Reduce Emissions from Deforestation and Forest Degradation.* Washington, DC: World Bank.

———. 2006e. *Protecting and Improving the Global Commons: 15 Years of the World Bank Group Global Environmental Facility Program.* Washington, DC: World Bank.

———. 2007a. *Quality of Supervision in FY05–06 (QSA7).* Quality Assurance Group. Washington, DC: World Bank.

———. 2007b. *Focus on Results: The IDA14 Results Measurement System and Direction for IDA15.* International Development Association / Operations Policy and Country Services Department. Washington, DC: World Bank.

———. 2007c. Note from the President of the World Bank, Robert Zoellick, for the 76th Meeting of the Development Committee. October 19, World Bank, Washington, DC.

———. 2007d. *Global Public Goods: A Framework for the Role of the World Bank.* Global Programs and Partnerships (GPP). Washington, DC: World Bank.

———. 2007e. *Meeting the Challenges of Global Development: A Long-Term Strategic Exercise for the World Bank Group.* Washington, DC: World Bank.

———. 2007f. *Sector Implementation Strategy: Third Review.* Operations Policy and Country Services Delivery Management. Washington, DC: World Bank.

———. 2007g. *Focus on Sustainability 2005/2006.* Washington, DC: World Bank.

———. 2007h. *Clean Energy for Development Investment Framework: The World Bank Group Action Plan.* Washington, DC: World Bank.

———. 2007i. *A Brief History of the Prototype Carbon Fund: The PCF 1997—2007, Pioneers in a Decade of Change.* Carbon Finance Unit. Washington, DC: World Bank.

———. 2007j. *Carbon Finance for Sustainable Development: 2007*. Washington, DC: World Bank.

———. 2007k. *Healthy Development: The World Bank Strategy for Health, Nutrition, and Population Results*. Washington, DC: World Bank.

———. 2007l. *IDA and Climate Change: Making Climate Action Work for Development*. Washington, DC: World Bank.

———. 2007m. *Global Public Goods: A Framework for the Role of the World Bank*. Report no. DC2007-0020. Background report for the Development Committee, World Bank, Washington, DC.

———. 2008a. *Annual Report on Portfolio Performance – 2007*. Quality Assurance Group. Washington, DC: World Bank.

———. 2008b. *Quality at Entry in FY06–07 (QEA8)*. Quality Assurance Group. Washington, DC: World Bank.

———. 2008c. *Additions to IDA Resources: Fifteenth Replenishment. IDA: The Platform for Achieving Results at the Country Level:* Report from the Executive Directors of the International Development Association to the Board of Governors. Approved by the Executive Directors of IDA, February 28. Washington, DC: World Bank.

———. 2008d. "Consultation Draft on Climate Investment Funds." Washington, DC: World Bank.